MW00790356

How to Sell Beer on the Bus

& gas processing plants around the world

ISBN-13: 978-1-951700-07-2
LCCN: 2020902729

Every effort has been made to trace the ownership of all
copyrighted material included in this publication. Any errors
that may occur are inadvertent and will be corrected in
subsequent additions, provided notification is sent to the
publisher.

How to Sell Beer on the Bus
& gas processing plants around the world

a collection of stories about Thomas H. Russell

Mandy Jordan

DEDICATED TO:

Ann Genevieve & Harold Edward Russell

PRAY ST·PATRICK FOR US.

CHRIST BESIDE ME,

CHRIST BEFORE ME,

CHRIST BEHIND ME,

CHRIST WITHIN ME,

CHRIST BENEATH ME,

CHRIST ABOVE ME.

– St. Patrick, Bishop of Ireland

Pull up a camp chair, sit by the fire, and hear the tale of a lad from Tulsa, Oklahoma, from his humble beginnings to his retirement.

Thomas Harold Russell was born to build business, family, and friendships. He sees potential in all people. He can find the positive in any situation, and his greatest possession is his sense of humor.

One can't help but feel his fatherly love, seek the flame of his advice, and bask in the glow of his presence. He has been a pioneer in the gas processing business, traveled the world, and even ridden the bull at Gilley's!

Don't deal with crooks.

– Calvin McKee

Table of Contents

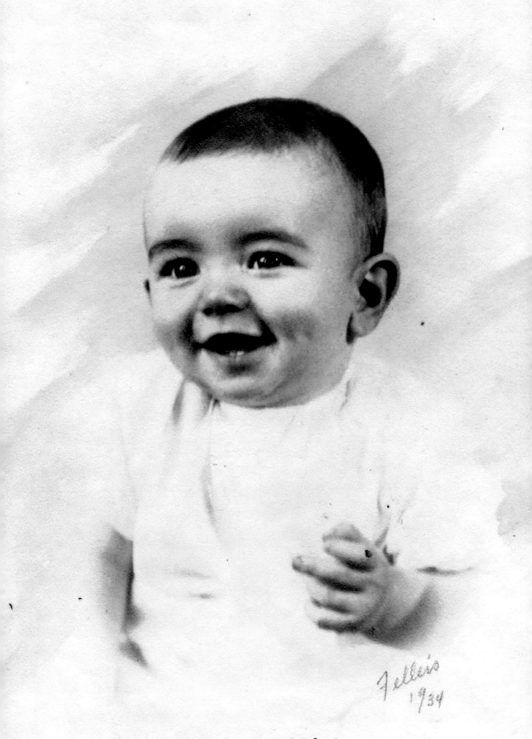

Has Tommy learned his lesson yet?

– Marquette Sister

Chapter 1
EARLY LIFE

Beer

What seemed like a typical day at the little house quickly changed with the ring of the telephone.

"Has Tommy learned his lesson yet?"

"What are you talking about, sister?" his mother, Ann, asked. It turned out Tommy had been expelled from school because of a fight between two boys during a school field trip. The beer Tommy had sold them on the bus en route had fueled the brawl!

This was news to his parents and his four older siblings, since he was still getting up every morning, putting on his school uniform, and heading out the door. A simple, nonchalant turn in the other direction took him to the pool hall to wait out the hours of the school day. Each day he was up and out, only to repeat the routine.

Tommy was born in 1933 during the Great Depression, the Dust Bowl, and if that weren't enough, World War II looming on the horizon. The Russell family and everyone else were struggling to make it. Fifteen million people were unemployed. Prohibition had put a demand on alcohol. Sacramental wine was still permitted for religious purposes. Drug stores were allowed to sell whiskey as "medicine," which was used to treat everything from toothaches to the flu.

With a physician's prescription, a pint of hard liquor could be legally purchased every ten days. Or, for a nickel and a handshake, you could get a bottle of brew from Tommy. He had found his father's old crockpot and bottle capper in the basement. He scrounged around in trash bins for discarded bottles to wash and reuse. After obtaining the recipe for malt, sugar, and yeast, Tommy was in the beer-making business. It would take him about a week to make a fresh batch, ready for sale.

After Ann hung up the phone, she put on her tattered overalls and went searching for Tommy's first processing plant. Ever so dedicated to her family and her community, she searched high and low until she found a small, dirty crawl space in the basement. Wedged inside she found his booming beer business in full operation. She cleaned herself up, regained her composure, and made dinner.

"How was school today?" Ann asked the children, as she typically did while they were gathered around the dinner table. The children knew not to pick up a fork until Ann was seated and grace was said.

"Oh, fine. I had a test," Tommy casually answered.

"Did you pass?" Ann inquired.

"Yep!" he replied with confidence.

"Was it about how much beer you sold today?" his mom quipped.

It got really quiet as all eyes darted around the table. Not a single clank of a utensil could be heard.

Suddenly, there was a loud commotion as Tommy's brother Joseph somersaulted backward out of his chair and right through the screen door, landing in the yard. All the siblings sprang to their feet and ran out to console Joseph. He had received a swift backhand from Harold, their father.

"What did Joseph do? What happened? What did he do?" they all asked, startled. Apparently, he was making a noise while he chewed.

Tommy's brewery business was capped. It turned out the Germans were destined to make the best beer. However, his entrepreneurial spirit stayed strong, and he was always working, working hard. This was a concept Harold and Ann had instilled in all their children. Times were tough, needless to say, and it required long hours for Harold to keep his family and his parents (along with his brother, sister-in-law, and their son for a time) afloat.

ONG

Oklahoma oil history began in 1897 after a huge column of oil erupted from a well near Bartlesville. Harold worked as an accountant with Oklahoma Natural Gas for over twenty-five years. He even received a gold watch for his service. During

Harold Russell

the Depression, his responsibilities and salary were greatly reduced. After work, Harold was a regular at the local McNellie's Irish Pub. He had served in the navy during World War I aboard the *USS Rhode Island* as a radio operator. He was a very no-nonsense, militarily disciplined, stern taskmaster of a man. The kids knew to mind their manners. He was a good provider and the love of Ann's life.

FAMILY FROM EAST TO WEST

All or some of the family at a time would often travel back to Chicago and Wisconsin to see relatives. Tom's older sister, Patricia, was working with Skelly Oil Company at the time and was the letter writer of the group. In one dated 1945, she speaks of having to buy a "good but expensive" lunch at the Brown-Dunkin tearoom, since their mother was away visiting relatives in Chicago, after leaving "a million instructions," and would usually pack everyone's lunches. Brown-Dunkin also had a department store inside what is now the First Place tower at Fourth and Main Street. They sold "special luncheons" for fifty cents, and models would go from table to table, tempting patrons with the latest fashion.

Harold was left with his older three daughters as the "culinary artists" in charge. He commented, "Well, this is a fine arrangement. What gives here?" If the girls had time to cook at all (after going out to Skyline), they first had to figure out grocery shopping for under two dollars, and all would gain an appreciation for Ann, as they were dependent on her cooking and caretaking. The goldfish would have to settle for a few breadcrumbs, because "we don't have the foggiest idea where Tommy hid their food" and "Mary is procrastinating a hop to Kress's (a five-and-dime store) for fish food." However, always looking out for her little brother, Patricia wrote, "I am enclosing my last dollar. Tell him not to spend it *all* at Art's."

* * *

At about seven years of age, Tommy would stay on his cousins James and Francis's farm in Wisconsin to work for up to six weeks at a time. Ann would arrange this to satisfy Tommy's desire to live on a farm. They would give him jobs such as feeding the pigs, carrying buckets of water, and other chores around the farm. This was where

6

he developed a deep passion for working the land. The others would stay with Aunt Regis. Harold got two weeks of vacation a year. Sometimes there was time to collect the family in the green Buick to attend the World's Fair. The family also had a brown Dodge for a time, but always only one vehicle between them. This would frequently require traveling by Greyhound bus.

OIL, OKLAHOMA, & ORCUTT

After the Civil War, many African-Americans and Native Americans migrated south to the "promised land," escaping slavery and religious persecution. They often settled together because of close relations, but more importantly the need for mutual protection and economic security. Together they formed cohesive and prosperous farms that could support businesses. Soon the Greenwood District downtown was thriving! It didn't take long for the persecutors to catch up.

T.D. Rice, of English descent, would travel around, dressing up as a black "Jim Crow" figure and acting in a very degrading manner. He claimed George Washington

had been a friend of his father's. Immediately following the ratification of the 13th Amendment, freeing four million slaves, Jim Crow laws were passed and unfortunately lasted for a hundred years. Former Confederate soldiers' sons had a lot of political power, the Ku Klux Klan was active, and people *still* protested "in his own likeness, after his image." This continued until the 36th President, Lyndon B. Johnson, in 1964 finished what John F. Kennedy had started.

* * *

Oklahoma was opened for general settlement around 1890, and the "Sooners" came for ranching and farming. Four years after oil was discovered in Oklahoma, it was found in Tulsa and surrounding areas in 1901. This attracted more oilmen from the East Coast, many of whom were Irish-Catholic.

* * *

The *Tulsa World* featured a story in 1987 asking "what do a three-foot alligator, a duck named Charley, and a fifty-seven-piece silverware set have in common? All have ended up in Tulsa's historic Swan Lake!" This spring-fed lake was a cattle watering hole. The area was an eight-hundred-acre homestead allotted to Anna Orcutt and her children, members of the Creek Indian tribe. Orcutt at the time was Tulsa's first and only park. It also had a movie theatre, playground, open-air dance pavilion, covered swimming pool, and amusement rides. Charley and the gator just showed up one day, and the silver was found when the lake was drained for reconstruction and treasure hunting. The early Tulsans came here to fish, have picnics, and go boating. Orcutt sold his part and lake to businessman and realtor E. J. Brennan in 1917. He renamed it Swan Lake and donated it to the city.

Catholic Community

In 1914 the Holy Family Cathedral was built on Eighth and Boulder after a priest had made several visits to Tulsa to celebrate Mass in private residences. It was built by hand for the community of Creek Indians and African-Americans, although all races were admitted. It was this Parish (and the First Presbyterian Church) that opened its doors during the devastating 1921 Tulsa Race Riots. The total population of Tulsa at that time was only fifteen thousand, four thousand of whom were members of Holy Family.

Little Tommy, dressed as a priest, with his siblings.

Holy Family provided refuge in their basement for victims to sleep, eat, take baths, and change clothes. The sisters took in at least 25 orphaned babies. The days after they risked being burned down, they served 253 meals.

Parishioners of the Guess family protected the 19-year-old falsely accused Dick Rowland. They hid out with him in the McNulty baseball park. The Catholic Church released a statement "we are all children of God."

The riot was largely omitted from local, state, and national history.

Another Parish would soon be needed. Sisters came from other states to teach the locals English using Sears catalogs. The locals were also given jobs at the Parish and the school. While they worked, worshiped, and learned, they most importantly were empowered to maintain their cultures and identities. It is the mother church of the Diocese of Tulsa and the seat of the Bishop Konderla.

A Catholic couple in 1917 sold their square block and two-story home on the corner of 16th and Quincy, where they had raised their nine children, for $17,000. The home was built in 1910, just three years after Oklahoma became a state. When it was first built, there was no electricity, only gaslights. This would be the site of Christ the King Parish (Sacred Heart) and Marquette School. They taught all grades up to high school, until Bishop Kelley was built in 1964. In Tommy's old football photographs, you can see a field behind him that is now the pre-K, as well as his team kneeling at the altar rail before their games.

Roaring Twenties

Harold and Ann were simple, hardworking farmers who met and married in Chicago and honeymooned at Niagara Falls. Around 1928, they were sent southwest for ONG's expansion project. They were in Tulsa just one year later when the stock market crashed and mobility was halted for many. Harold lost his job and had to find work for half his previous salary. Unable to afford mortgage payments, they moved into a humble house at 16th and Trenton. They paid rent, gave thanks for all their blessings, and welcomed five kids. Ann attended Mass daily at Christ the King. She was involved in many women's groups at the Parish, and Harold was an usher. All five kids graduated from Marquette School. This home remained in the Russell family, thanks to Joseph, until 1979.

Ann held the family together. She always had dinner on the table, the kids in church, and the house chores done, and no matter what, she made it work.

One Thanksgiving dinner, Tommy noticed more than two drumsticks going around the table. He had attended class enough to know that turkeys had only two legs.

"How did we get more than two drumsticks this year?" he asked.

It became eerily quiet at the dinner table. Tommy jumped up and ran out to the garage. Sure enough, his beloved pet chicken had just been served up with gravy! Tommy hasn't had much of an appetite for chicken since.

* * *

Besides serving as an altar boy, Tommy worked several jobs: setting the pins at the bowling alley, sacking people's groceries at Roger's Store, and a newspaper route. His sisters would ride the bus downtown to work as secretaries. Joseph sought work in carpentry. There was no allowance for chores in those days. Everyone had to pull their weight and fend for the family good. It was normal, as no one in the neighborhood was living *fancy*.

Tommy remembers, "We never thought we were poor or felt sorry for ourselves. We counted our blessings." Knowing firsthand the persecution and prejudice against Irish-Catholics, the Russell family had sympathy for the Jewish, African-Americans, and Native Americans (the biggest targets at the time). "I never understood why? What was the big problem? Why did people hate them so much? It didn't make sense to me. We are all people," Tommy would ponder. "I see them working hard too," he would challenge.

Racial relations were severely damaged, and prejudices ran deep. All the ethnicities had to stick together and close to their faith.

"I'd really like the name 'Tony' for my confirmation name!" Tommy exclaimed once at the table.

"Isn't that an Italian name, son?" Harold looked puzzled.

"I like it!" he responded.

"Your confirmation name will be Patrick," Harold said, determined, and that was the end of that conversation.

Delivering Newspapers

By the early 1940s, the draft for WWII was in effect for men eighteen years of age and up. Too young to enlist, Tommy sought various other jobs. Delivering papers required him to clock in at five in the morning before anyone else was up, and long before any breakfast. Sometimes he also had the four pm evening shift. He was paid only 30 cents an hour. At just twelve years old, he was determined to do his job well. He had the angles down pretty good, able to throw a paper like a football to a receiver. Except once when an incomplete pass crashed into the neon "Cain's Coffee" sign and shattered it to pieces, creating an explosion in the sky. Heat, rain, or snow was no matter, nor was the dark of the dawn, or the growling tummy of a growing boy. The job must get done.

During one route, the weight of the bags pulled the bike over and Tommy toppled over in the street. After picking himself up, he stood alone under the streetlight with his papers scattered all over the place, blowing in the wind. What did someone who could always find the good in a bad situation do? He sat down on the curb, picked up one of the papers, and used the opportunity to get caught up on the news. Crude oil prices had dropped to twenty-five cents a barrel, Prohibition was repealed (but not in Oklahoma), and phonograph record sales had plunged, as radio became the medium of entertainment.

On Fridays, he was required to return to all the homes to collect cash for the papers he had delivered. The money was due Saturday. This was also the savvy salesman's opportunity to rate customer satisfaction. "Are you happy with your subscription service, Mister?" With a lot of positive feedback and few cancellations, he was sure to be delivering more than a newspaper. In typical Tommy style, he was delivering service with value.

The challenge was not to spend all the profits at the pool hall Friday night! Tommy would sit at the kitchen table with all his bills and coins spread out to count. He knew that "happy customers" made for a "happy payday." About $1 per house per month was the cost of the service, with hopefully a few extra cents in tips. Ann would walk by and say, "Big butter and egg man." If he managed to have enough left over, he would treat himself to a nickel doughnut, which was a rare special treat for a boy who liked sweets. Sometimes he and his buddies would have to consolidate what little change they had and share a doughnut between them, each getting only one bite, but well worth it.

* * *

Tulsa World was founded in 1905 by locals and Republican activists, the Lorton family. The business was headquartered at 315 S. Boston Avenue and kept in the family for 100 years.

In the 1920s the paper was known for its opposition to the Ku Klux Klan which had unfortunately risen to local prominence during the aftermath of the riot.

The Russell family was known for their integrity. Once, Tommy accidentally picked up the wrong paycheck which was way more than he had earned. Despite the temptation to keep the money, Tommy confessed the mistake to his father.

"Take it back," Harold instructed. And that's exactly what Tommy got on his bicycle and did.

* * *

Entertainment in the neighborhood was playing hockey in the streets. Tommy and his friends would watch the Tulsa Oilers practice, then wait outside for the players to come out. If a player had cracked his stick, they would ask him for it. Eventually they had collected enough broken sticks, which they duct-taped back together, to form two teams. They had one tennis ball between them, and street hockey in the alley was their favorite pastime.

* * *

On one Halloween night, a police officer escorted Tommy home (as was the case a few other times). He and his pals had been roaming the neighborhood when he got the bright idea to shimmy up a pole and unscrew the light bulbs. Why? Why not? Parked right down the street was a cop on patrol. Ann spoke with the policeman at the door who released his clasp on the back of Tommy's collar. Ann shut the door and reached out for the same collar, but the chase was on!

"How did your mom discipline you?" people would later ask him.

Ann, Harold, and Little Tommy

Mary Ellen, Patricia Ann,
Eileen, Joseph, and Tommy

"I don't know. She could never catch me!" he would snicker.

This proved to be useful training, as Tommy played football all through school. Besides being a football player, he developed a lifelong enthusiasm for being a football fan. Swinney's Hardware store on 14th and Lewis had a little fuzzy TV in the window (no one had them in their homes at the time). Tommy and his buddies would gather around on the sidewalk to watch the games. "We couldn't hear it, but we could see the excitement, and sometimes we bet pennies on the game." NBC was the first network to cover an NFL game on October 22, 1939, between the Philadelphia Eagles and Brooklyn Dodgers. Six-year-old Tommy was hooked.

Russell family on a walking history tour in Ireland.

All eight of my great-grandparents were born in Ireland.

I'm proud of my Irish ancestry.

— Tom Russell

Chapter 2

IRISH HERITAGE

Fifth-Century Ireland

Pagan Irish pirates kidnapped a British lad named Patrick when he was just fourteen years old. He was starved, beaten, and enslaved in Ireland for six years, forced to herd sheep until he bravely escaped. In 418 AD, he converted to Catholicism and was ordained a priest in France, much to his polytheistic parents' disapproval, as it disqualified him for any inheritance. Fifteen years later, he returned to Ireland in March of 433. Patrick preached and converted all of Ireland. For forty years, he worked many miracles, living in poverty and enduring much suffering during his missionary work.

Using the three-leaf clover to explain the Triune God, he brought the Church (building 300 churches) and the

Sacraments (baptizing 100,000 people) to the country. He became the first Bishop of Ireland. He died on March 17, 461 in Ireland. For Jewish and Catholic believers, it was customary to recognize the passing of a significant person or event as a religious observance and a feast day in honor of them. St. Patrick's Day was celebrated with Mass and a feast of cabbage and bacon.

During this time, the people in Ireland lived in clans under kings, farming and grazing their livestock on their "verdant hills," and developing iron technology. They were in communion with the Bishop of Rome while maintaining their culture, language, and identity.

Fifteenth Century and Reformation

King Henry VIII of England's "Great Matter" was his desire to annul his marriage with the queen so he could marry his pregnant mistress in hopes of gaining a male heir. Pope Clement VII refused the king's petition because his behavior was against Church teaching. Henry was determined to legalize his wishes, so in 1534 he declared the Act of Supremacy. It demanded citizens put their faith in and pledge allegiance to the king alone, or be imprisoned for treason and possibly killed. He claimed he was "directed by God and not answerable to men." Many pledged their faith to the king to avoid losing their homes, land, and lives.

Starting in Dublin, Henry had monasteries (some hundreds of years old) dissolved and razed to the ground. Religious hospitals and schools were confiscated and their property sold off to fund his military campaigns. Clergy that refused to submit were charged with treason, executed on the spot, or starved to death in prison. Former priests or nuns who were forced to seek alternative vocations were "strictly forbidden ever to marry" under Henry's reign. Personal? Maybe just a little. Political? You could say so. Spiritually motivated? Don't think so. Protestantism was the king's new power play, mass-produced with the invention of the printing press.

Potatoes

In 1536, Spanish conquistadors introduced the potato (and the tomato) to County Cork. It quickly became the fourth largest staple, following rice, wheat, and maize.

It was much easier to grow than oats. Potatoes were considered to contain most of the vitamins needed for sustenance. One potato provided for ten people. If you asked Grandma Ann, though, "All the vitamins are in the peel, not the potato." They were served not only for dinner, but lunch and even breakfast.

Boxty on the griddle, boxty in the pan. If you can't make boxty, you'll never get your man.

By 1565, potato crops, Catholicism, and cattle ranching had made their way to the Americas via the Spaniards. Squanto, a Patuxet Indian and a Catholic, reached Massachusetts about five years before the Puritans. They reached the natives about fifty years before the Puritans did. The first Thanksgiving was actually a Catholic Mass on a feast day celebrated by Father Francisco Lopez, attended by Spaniards, Indians, and Pilgrims in 1619. Holy Communion is a celebration of a sacrament literally meaning thanksgiving. Later, President

Abraham Lincoln declared it a federal holiday in 1863, during the American Civil War. He called it, "A Day of Thanksgiving and Praise to our Beneficent Father who Dwelleth in the Heavens."

SIXTEENTH-CENTURY IRELAND AND THE SLAVE TRADE

England passed the Popery Act in 1698, placing a bounty of one hundred pounds on any priest's head. After years of British "lordship," only English and Scottish settlers could own land, not the Irish, who could only rent it. The landlords would charge the tenants heavy taxes and force them to farm for meager wages. Their crops and livestock were exported back to England. At the top of the political, economic, and social class were the English. Irish children as young as ten were taken as slaves, up to 100,000 during this time period alone. Sadly, the African slave trade was just beginning at this time too. Africa had been Catholic (due to the work of St. Alexandria of Egypt), skilled in agriculture, and possessed of a prosperous economy of trading shells and precious metals since the first century, while the Irish were still grunting and throwing rocks at each other.

Ireland quickly became the biggest source of human livestock for English merchants to the New World. Africans sold for fifty pounds sterling a person. Irish slaves came much cheaper at only five pounds sterling each, so it wasn't a crime to whip, brand, or even beat them to death. "Breeding" Irish women to African men produced "mulatto" women and children who could bring more profit. The legal tender was gold and silver and goods valued by British pounds. One such "good" was tobacco leaves, sometimes substituted with the receipt for it, leading to paper money later in the eighteenth century.

Michelle Obama in her 2016 speech at the Democratic National Convention in Philadelphia got reamed for saying the phrase "built by slaves" when referring to the 1792 building of the White House. But indeed, trained, enslaved immigrants from Ireland, Scotland, Africa, and other European nations built it. They were given the "privilege" to assist the *Free*masons, a fraternal, secret society from England.

SEVENTEENTH-CENTURY COLONIES

Oh, come on now. The British do make the best tea, the Beatles made the best rock, Shakespeare wrote the best plays, and who doesn't love fish and chips! True, however, to say that the Puritans were fleeing England, getting loans, separating their families, sometimes leaving their children behind, and risking death aboard "coffin" ships because it was still "too Catholic" doesn't make sense. They hadn't done that for the last 1,000 to 1,300 years, when the country actually was Catholic. The Puritans fled England because of the tyranny of the King.

The pilgrims were poor, uneducated, non-religious, few in number, and the first to flee. The Puritans were England's elite, well-educated and looking for a "Calvinistic" utopia. Both had become dependent on the monarch and had difficulty fending for themselves. Neither was subject to the same "disinfection" criteria as the enslaved Irish and Africans were, so smallpox and diphtheria were a problem.

In the colonies, propaganda was spread, speeches were given, and heresy was taught as fact in schools.

Eight of the thirteen colonies had "official" Protestant community houses set up. They enforced very strict religious observance. Laws mandated that everyone had to attend and pay moderate taxes that funded the salaries of the ministers. Anyone caught preaching any variation of Protestantism was persecuted for disloyalty to the king and often killed. In all thirteen of the English colonies, it was actually illegal to be Catholic for one hundred and eighty years, since the first pilgrim set foot on colonial soil.

The slaves in the North were producing lumber, fish, iron, copper, and lead. The middle colonies were mostly about corn, cattle, wheat, and pork. This was where the Scotch-Irish typically settled, such as in the Carolinas, which also eventually produced Andrew Jackson and Ronald Reagan. The South, with its humid, fertile soil, was producing the cash crops: tobacco, rice, cotton, sugar, and indigo.

If a Catholic was caught *attempting* to hold any political office, they were fined 1,000 pounds of tobacco. Two priests were caught with the Holy Bible instead of King James's book, so they were murdered in the street by being tarred and feathered. Other priests had four days to leave or suffer the same fate.

Celebrating the Sacraments and Mass had to be done in complete privacy. Catholics were called "papist," and practicing was "popery." They were hated, ridiculed, had no legal rights, were enslaved, and were given the most dangerous jobs: coal mines, railroads, bridges, roads, and canals. It was a common joke that "Irish were buried under the rails." Fines were levied if you were caught sending your child overseas to receive an education. In 1768 Boston-born Samuel Adams stated, "I did verily believe, as I do still, that much more is to be dreaded from the growth of popery in America, than from the Stamp Act, or any other acts destructive of civil rights."

THE REVOLUTIONARY WAR (1775-1783)

Colonists were growing increasingly disenchanted with the loyalist British, who were backed by Germany at the time. They began to reject and rebel against such heavy taxation with no say in the matter. So they threw their tea in the sea! George Washington, backed by Spain and France, was appointed commander in chief and led the patriots to independence. He became the first President six years after the war ended in 1789. The colonies still had a ways to go. Washington was a master *Free*mason (since his promotion at the Masonic lodge in Virginia in 1753), the slaves weren't free for another seventy-eight years.

* * *

There were two Catholic signers of the Constitution in 1787: Ireland-born Thomas Fitzsimons, and Dan Carroll (of Irish descent) from Maryland. Carroll's family motto was "Strong in Faith and War." He moved for the document to say, "By the people" instead of "by the legislator." He also moved to make the colonies not declare a state religion, like England, upholding free will.

His brother Fr. John Carroll, who was highly recommended by Benjamin Franklin, was the first Bishop of the United States, residing in Maryland. He founded Georgetown University. It's the oldest Catholic university in the U.S., founded in 1789. Male relatives of Tom's would later be able to graduate from colleges such as Loyola in Chicago, founded in 1870.

Bill of Rights

In 1791, the Second Amendment "Right of the people to keep and bear arms" was ratified. This law was *not* intended for hunting. It was so the English in the colonies could defend themselves and their country from the King of England. It was a result of the 1689 English common law of Sir William Blackstone, a London judge. It stated specifically "That the subjects which are Protestant may have Arms for their Defense suitable to their Condition and as allowed by Law." King William III of Orange intended this so his subjects could defend *him*, not themselves.

The concept presents itself first in the Holy Bible. Luke 22:36 is one of several Scriptures where our Lord indicates the legitimacy of the right to self-defense, telling his disciples to "buy a sword and arm themselves." The Russells were going to take "bearing arms" (our biblical and Second Amendment right) to a whole new level. Take that, Clint Eastwood!

Crossing the Atlantic in the 1800s

By the 1840s in Ireland, the tenant peasant farmers' land holdings were so small that no crop other than potatoes would suffice to feed a family. They survived only by small earnings as seasonal migrant laborers in England and Scotland. The potato blight (fungal plant disease) actually originated in Mexico and spread to Europe. Mass starvation and disease claimed a million lives and caused a million more to leave. If one survived the famine, there was only one other thing worse than being Irish, and that was being Catholic.

The British government had placed harsh restrictions on Irish immigration to Canada. Although the fare was a bit less to Canada, they didn't want *any* Catholics there. The typical pattern was for the eldest son to go first by ship. Being usually unskilled, he would work for meager wages as a laborer however he could.

The first of the Kennedy clan to arrive in Boston was a laborer named Patrick Kennedy from Wexford, Ireland. Five generations later, John F. Kennedy, the Massachusetts-born 35th president, would reform American civil rights.

Ship fare was half the annual income of a laborer. It took a minimum of twelve weeks to cross the Atlantic Ocean, with a 10% mortality rate. Where the present-day Statue of Liberty comes into view, the rest of the passage was by ferry or barge. It took up to five hours to go through legal and medical screening. Passengers and bags were "disinfected" or sometimes separated and sent back.

For centuries, British laws had deprived Ireland's Catholics of their rights to worship, vote, speak their language, and own land, horses, or guns. They were even denied food, with the famine raging. Armed guards escorted convoys of wheat, oats, and barley to England, filling 4,000 vessels during that period. The ships were also loaded with peas, onions, rabbits, salmon, oysters, honey, and butter. Cattle, sheep, and pigs were still being exported plentifully as well. There was plenty of food, but only for the English.

Crowley Comes to the U.S.

Ann's great-grandfather Patrick Crowley was the first from her clan to arrive, in 1849. The origin of the name Crowley means "hard hero." He was the oldest of five from County Waterford. They were poor peasant farmers who had managed to have their children baptized in secret. Patrick used his last pennies saved

for the transit. Allowed only eighteen inches of space aboard the dark, crowded ship named *The Swan*, he

Patrick Crowley   *The Swan*

was determined to survive. He was twenty-five years old, although he is listed as only twenty because passengers over twenty-one had to pay a higher fare.

He had learned shoemaking in Ireland but wasn't able or allowed to find work in that trade in New York. He worked as a butcher until he could save enough to travel west. He made his way by train from New York to Chicago (where Tom's parents Ann and Harold would later meet), then to Wisconsin, where he built a log cabin with his bare hands. He knew to head for the hills, literally 1,000 miles away from the coast. Out there, settlers were allowed to occupy federal land, improve it, and buy it at a reduced price. What a deal…for the government.

A second wave of Crowleys came aboard the ship *Constitution* and worked in apple orchards in New York to earn their westward train fare. Patrick would travel back from his cabin in Wisconsin by covered wagon, pulled by oxen, ninety arduous miles to Chicago to meet the train in order to escort his relatives west. He obtained the title to his land in 1857 after eight years of hard labor building cabins for others. He lived till the age of 90! The area was nicknamed Crowley Ridge.

Abraham Lincoln

Lincoln wrote a letter to the nation in 1855 that read, "When the know-nothings get control, it [the Declaration] will read 'all men are created equal except Negroes, foreigners and Catholics.'" He was born into poverty in a one-room cabin in the woods and was a self-taught man, even learning to read on his own. Nicknamed Honest Abe, he was on his way to becoming our sixteenth president. The states were on their way to Civil War, and Tommy's ancestors were going to be a part of it.

Know-nothings had gained political power in 1854. Their focus was the German and Irish immigrants, mainly. They closed saloons on Sundays. The penalty was six months in prison for serving one glass of beer. They also opposed Chinese immigration and barred all immigrants from city jobs in Chicago. *Public* schools were required to teach King James's book. Naturalization was raised from five years to twenty-one years. They appointed a well-funded committee to find immorality among Catholics and to spread anti-Catholic propaganda.

"Bloody Monday" was a violent riot. It took place when armed know-nothings blocked Catholics from voting. They caught a German priest going to visit a sick person and murdered him in the street. In 1836 the anti-Catholic, fabricated book *Awful Disclosures of Maria Monk* sold over 300,000 copies, making her a considerable profit.

The protestors in Canada demanded an investigation into the claims. An inquiry found no evidence to support her writings, though many refused to accept the findings and believed her filth.

Russell Comes to the U.S.

Matthew Patrick Russell and his wife, Mary, (also poor tenant farmers) from near Dublin were the first of the Russell clan to arrive in 1859, landing in New York aboard the *SS Lucy Thompson*. All eight of their children were born on the East Coast. Within the next six years,

Matthew Russell

SS Lucy Thompson

all four great-grandparents and many other relatives made the journey. While they endured the long voyage, they clung to faith, hope, charity, and each other.

Thomas Russell

Meanwhile, Charles Darwin, an English Protestant, came up with his Evolution of Natural Selection "theory" in 1859. He believed that "English eyes appeared superior to foreigners.'" He drew descriptions of African and Irish people with violent ape heads and human bodies or vice versa. He stated, "The civilized races of man will almost certainly exterminate and replace the savage races throughout the world." Suddenly everything Catholic was "an evil plot."

AMERICAN CIVIL WAR (1861-1865)

The war was set off by the election of Abraham Lincoln. He attended Protestant services with his wife and

children but never officially joined. With so many
Chinese, Italians, Germans, British, Africans, Spanish,
and Irish all living together, forming friendships,
marriages, and babies, the whole poorly planned "pure"
thing wasn't going over well. The Africans in the six
Northern Union states had finally had enough, and
rightfully so. They rallied under the banner of General
Ulysses S. Grant. The seven Southern Confederate

Lithograph by Kurz & Allis

41

states, heavily dependent on slave labor, didn't agree and separated themselves under general Robert E. Lee. Sadly, many were spreading the anti-Catholic message. "…I was educated to enmity toward everything that is Catholic," Mark Twain said. "No spiritual reason, just hate just because."

The secret society of the Ku Klux Klan had already formed in the southern states. They were Scottish- or English-descended male protestors (women didn't join till 1920) who were terrorizing Catholics and other foreigners. They believed the only "pure 100% Americanism" were the English. They wore bedsheets with eyeholes cut out to reject the "superstitious" belief in the Father, the Son, and the Holy Ghost. They burned the cross, which was the only sacred symbol (sometimes just two small sticks twined together) the immigrants brought with them from overseas.

Abraham Lincoln, who had developed a reputation for integrity, asked the question, "Shall it be peace or the sword?" Registration records show that a couple of Russells and Crowleys applied but couldn't serve officially in the army. However, 150,000 Irishman did fight with the Union for civil and religious freedom. Over 90,000 were from Wisconsin.

The Irish made up over fifty Union regiments. Earning just $13 a month, and with a high risk of dying, these soldiers helped win civil freedom for all. With the spiritual guidance of priests, the Africans, Irish, and other Catholics set up areas to celebrate Mass every morning together in private before battle. This inspired the song "Kelly's Irish Brigade." It makes one wonder what all our ancestors experienced.

If you haven't seen the 1989 movie *Glory*, put it on your next rainy-day list. Matthew Broderick portrays colonel commander Robert Gould Shaw of the first all-African regiment. Massachusetts born Colonel Shaw was a Roman Catholic, but of course Hollywood left that part out. The 54th volunteer infantry were paid less than $10 a month. Morgan Freeman and Denzel Washington give notable performances. Many of the volunteers were from the Joy Street House. Although they were Protestant, they weren't English and therefore not welcome in English places. It was this infantry that turned the tide for winning the Civil War.

Meanwhile, in 1862, protestant Anglo-Saxon Thomas Nast was earning $20,000 (equivalent to $500,000 today) at just sixteen years of age, drawing political cartoons for *Harper's Weekly*. He won awards for Best Cartoons on International Affairs, such as one of his most famous ones, depicting Roman Catholic clergy as crocodiles invading America's shore to devour the white, black, Indian, and Chinese schoolchildren under an upside-down Old Glory. A nicely dressed boy with a King James book in his pocket is standing in front of the other children to "protect" them. The radical Republican white supremacist.

Nast is also credited with inventing Santa Claus and flying reindeer to replace Christ's Mass. His first depiction is of a man wearing a blue jacket pattern with

Cartoon by Thomas Nast

white stars, pants with red and white stripes (much like his Uncle Sam character). Claus (meaning people of victory) is holding a puppet with a rope around his neck thought to be president Jefferson Davis. This political cartoon character (who has become a diety) had nothing to do with a bishop from Turkey.

His most offensive cartoon is of two white men shaking hands to congratulate each other in front of a burning school grieving black parents over their dead child with a man hung from a tree in the background.

Ohio-born Ulysses S. Grant's wife was Protestant. He attended service occasionally with her, but never officially joined. He was a very skilled equestrian and a very strategic military genius. Grant and Lincoln were champions of civil rights! Now we can proudly say America is the "Land of the Free because of the Brave"! As well as proudly say African-Americans, Spanish-Americans, German-Americans, Italian-Americans, and Irish-Americans. It was the immigrants, the slaves, and the outcasts who won America's freedom for all. American soil was fertilized with foreigners' blood.

There is truth to the claim that any position of power was discriminatory in colonial America—police, fire, military, political leader, teachers and preachers!

The immigrants are the ones who turned Old Glory right side up and fended off the wolves, reptiles, and the intellectual inconsistency of humans.

Lincoln was assassinated in 1865 (only five days after his victory) by a know-nothing Anglo-Saxon named John Booth. Andrew Johnson assumed the presidency. Unfortunately, the animosity didn't just disappear. Bias ran deep, and states continued on with "slave codes," using their power and traditions to continue their discrimination. U.S. Immigration passed a law in 1893 increasing the number of questions for Irish immigrants to thirty-one, including asking if they had the "ability to read/write, did they have at least $25, and have they been to prison?"

The signs "No Irish Need Apply" still hung over job postings. They crammed into shantytowns and white British abandoned those areas of fear for violence, disease, and poverty. "White flight" is a real phenomenon.

* * *

Tommy's parents (not yet married) were in Chicago for the horrible 1919 Klan race riot, which killed thirty-eight people. A single Harold was also in Tulsa working when the Klan reared their ugly heads again in the horrific 1921 Tulsa Race Riot, killing about three hundred black people. This has been the only time in American history when American airplanes dropped bombs…on Americans! The Klan worked out of their Beno Hall, meaning: "be no Negro, be no Jew, be no Catholic, be no immigrant." Their national spokesperson (an, *ahem*, "minister") gave a speech calling the tragedy a "huge success and the best thing that ever happened to Tulsa."

During the riot, officials deputized any white man who had served in the military on the spot. This included Harold. Tommy remembers stories his father told about being in the crowd as "a mob was trying to hang a black man from a billboard…. It was complete chaos everywhere." Luckily that innocent person was spared, but many others were not. Tulsa's current mayor, G.T. Bynum, has rightfully named the incident a race "massacre." He has authorized search and recovery of victims for proper burial, addressing the hundred-year-old "well-earned lack of trust." As you have read, these wounds go back 243 years for America.

Segregation wasn't outlawed until the 1954 Supreme Court case Oliver Brown (a black preacher) vs. Board of Education (in Topeka, KS). Six years later, Martin Luther King, Jr. visited Tulsa on July 28, 1960. The activist stated, "We must all live together as brothers or we will die together as fools." Tom's brother Joseph would later comment, "Segregation was just taken for granted. It was normal everywhere you went."

Building Family
in America

Tommy's parents, Ann and Harold, met at a Catholic social event, which was the common method for Jewish and Catholic believers alike. Creed was what mattered to them,

Tommy in his Marquette Letterman jacket.

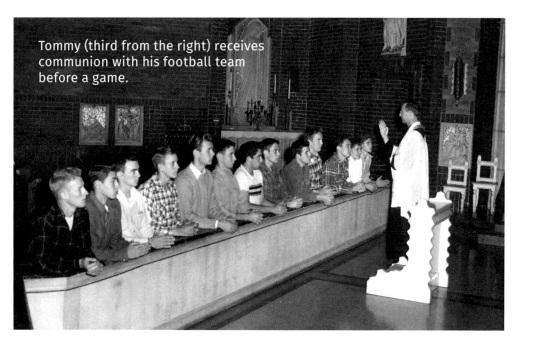

Tommy (third from the right) receives communion with his football team before a game.

not what country you were from. It is still what matters today. That is how Tommy and his sisters would meet their future spouses: Patricia (Calvin McKee), Mary Ellen (Bob Bradley), Eileen (Bob Funk). Joseph was ordained a Catholic priest.

When Calvin was courting Pat, he would drive his motorcycle to the little house at 16th and Trenton. "My mother and father wouldn't allow her to ride on it, so he would park it so they could hop the bus to the Orcutt Park picture show for "date night." *Casablanca*, with Humphrey Bogart and Ingrid Bergman, was the hit at the time.

Tommy's sisters had a system of getting a certain distance from the house before rolling the top of their skirts to make them shorter, and they would apply more makeup that had been smuggled out. "I was in a gang," Pat would proclaim, beaming. "Nobody messed with me."

Always one to capitalize on opportunities, a fourteen-year-old Tommy would spend the evening coasting down the hill on Calvin's motorcycle, and then with help from other neighborhood kids, push it back up for another go.

* * *

During what was supposed to be a nice garden party at the house, Tommy, always the prankster, thought an excellent accessory to all the tables of food set up in the backyard would be his model airplane engines. After he clamped one to each table, he went along and fired up all the little gasoline engines. It was so loud that none of the guests could hear each other over the roaring sound. Ann chased him around (but couldn't catch the quarterback) and yelled for him to shut them off! But once they are fueled up and started, they have to run out of gas before they'll stop. It

#81, Tommy's Blocking Pose

turned out Tommy would never run out of gas, as he ended up building two successful gas processing companies.

* * *

Tommy's brothers-in-law went to serve in World War II. "The only thing we have to fear is fear itself," said Franklin D. Roosevelt during one of his evening Fireside Chats. He was the first president to be broadcast over the radio, reaching millions. He chatted about the Emergency Banking Act, the Depression, New Deal initiatives, and WWII.

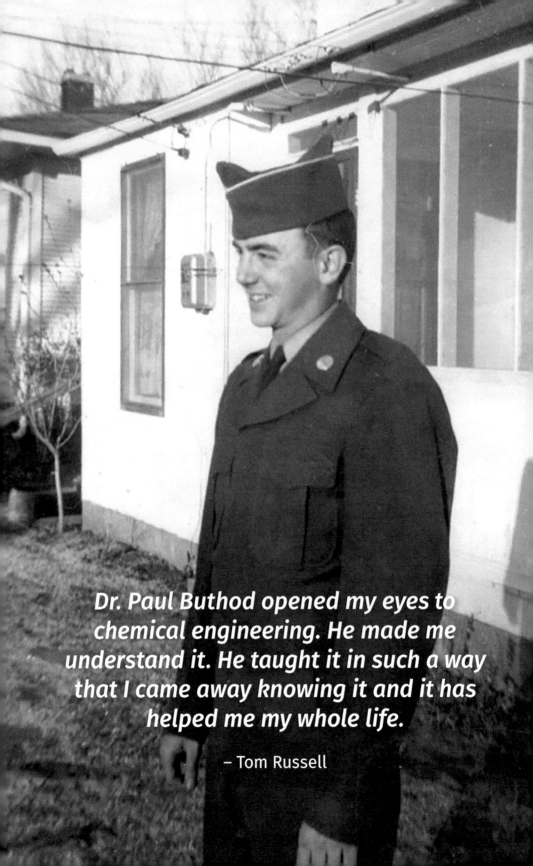

Dr. Paul Buthod opened my eyes to chemical engineering. He made me understand it. He taught it in such a way that I came away knowing it and it has helped me my whole life.

– Tom Russell

Chapter 3

THE ARMY
and UNIVERSITY

Tom graduated Marquette High School in 1951 with
no definite career plans but well prepared for higher
education. The world was struggling to survive the ravages
of World War II. Every day, it was on the news. It was the
deadliest conflict in human history: the only use of nuclear
weapons, the horrendous genocide of the Holocaust, and
over 65 million fatalities. Included in the massacre were
six million Jewish people and about 5,000 priests and
nuns who perished in concentration camps.

Thousands of churches and monasteries were
confiscated, closed, or destroyed. Priceless works of
religious art and sacred objects were lost forever. Priests
were targeted as part of an overall evil effort to destroy

Polish culture. When the war was finally over, with devastating consequences, the Soviet Union and the United States were divided as rival "superpowers," which led to the Cold War for the next forty years.

All three of Tom's brothers-in-law made it back home…hence the Baby Boom! Tom spent a lot of time with veterans, hearing their stories about their experiences. Many veterans were finishing college on the G.I. Bill. The market became a seller's market. Families had to adapt to popular cultural changes, including purchasing TVs, opening credit card accounts, and buying mouse ears to wear while watching *The Mickey Mouse Club.*

It was important to Ann to host soldiers at their home for Thanksgiving dinners. "I got to sit and listen to all the stories and be around these guys who had traveled, served, and sacrificed…. My parents always cared for the soldiers and their families." This would later inspire Brian McKee (Tom's nephew) and Tom to host veterans for Dallas Cowboy football games on Thanksgiving holidays. They wanted to be sure veterans always had "a place at the table."

The population explosion created a huge demand for housing, transportation, facilities, food, and yes, oil and gas. The oil and gas business was thriving and expanding. Following the advice and in the footsteps of Calvin McKee, Tom began studying chemical engineering at the University of Tulsa. He got a job to help pay his tuition. Calvin introduced him to the chief engineer at his previous place of employment, Vulcan Steel, where he built pressure vessels and tanks. Tom began work as a draftsman there. He would go in at night after class and do his work, which suited a busy young college student.

Some nights, Tom would tiptoe through the house, upstairs, and out his bedroom window onto the roof. Down below would be about ten excited neighborhood kids who had gathered at the side of the house, all vying for the best position, elbowing and jumping up and down with arms outstretched as high as they could. They had to be cautious not to alert Grandma Ann to what was going on, as she would not approve.

"Drop it! Drop it!" the crowd would holler.

"Ready?" Tom would ask while holding his homemade parachute tied to a box of nuts and bolts to weight it. When he released it, it would soar through the air and float down to the eager crowd, sometimes blowing out into the street. To be the one to catch it was like getting the trophy. It would be snatched up and disappear, only to reappear at the next gathering, and everyone knew exactly where to go and what to do without saying a word.

PATERNAL ERA

During the fall semester of his freshman year at TU, Tom was heading out the door as usual to go to class and then work. He stopped under the streetlight where he had stood many times as a young boy, turned, and went back inside the house. For some unknown reason, Tom was compelled to sit on the side of Harold's bed and talk to him early that morning. They visited about general things for a while, which was a rare tender moment. Afterward, Tom stood up, walked out the door, and proceeded with his busy schedule. That would be the last time he ever talked to his father. Harold died later that same day from a sudden heart attack. It solidified in Tom never to put off the impulse to reach out for a moment of quality time with someone.

Tom's innate desire to help others went into overdrive. He looked to Calvin even more for mentorship. Calvin had already instinctively taken the young man under his wing. Because of the growing demands of the cost of living, tuition, plus the worsening situation of the Korean War, after two years of college, Tom decided to put his studies on hold to join the army. Like his mentor, Tom believed in defensive war only.

Having been too young to serve during WWII, he admired the veterans even though there was nothing glamorous about the horrors of war. Tom knew he must be one of the men who risked everything to stand against evil and fight for freedom—everyone's freedom.

Ann didn't know it yet, as she was grieving the love of her life. Ann's heart was crushed. They had been together from the start, and now it was time to be stronger. Gone was Father.

The Call of Duty

During the Cold War and at the suggestion of the U.S., Korea had been divided in two at the 39th parallel without their consent or consultation. The North was established as a socialist state under communist (Russian and

Chinese) rule. The South was a capitalist state under anti-communist (U.S.) rule. The conflict had escalated when the North invaded the South on June 25, 1950. Jet fighters confronted each other in air-to-air combat for the first time in history. Tom had studied physics in college, so he scored high on the test given by the army. Knowing how war affected a man and the risk to Tom's future, joining the armed forces was not part of the advice Tom's mentor had given him. And he was not pleased.

Tom sensed the familiar presence in the home and heard determined footsteps heading straight for him. He quickly swung around in his chair and pretended to be studying. The sound of every ever-closer stomp echoed Tom's pounding heart. Without seeing anything or hearing a single word spoken, Tom felt himself catapulted straight up in the air. His body was airborne out of his chair, and he came crashing down to the floor. Before he could even stand up, Calvin proceeded to pound the laundry off him. After Calvin hoped he had knocked some sense into the young lad, he turned and, in solemn silence, walked out of the house.

Lying on the floor battered and bruised but not broken, Tom knew the beating had hurt Calvin more than it had hurt him. And he was more determined than ever to prove himself worthy of joining the ranks, fighting for his country and freedom, and becoming a man. He got up, straightened his twisted shirt, and packed his bags for Albuquerque, New Mexico, to train in atomic weaponry. This would be the first, but not the last time, Tom would strike out on his own.

"Don't go, finish your school," Ann pleaded to her youngest and only child still left at home.

"I have to, Mother. Duty calls." And with that, Tom was gone.

ARMY

In April of 1954, Tom was sent to West Germany, where he was stationed with the 9th Ordinance Battalion. He served for two years, as an atomic weapons electronic assembly specialist. He still keeps his seven-page list of names and addresses of the men he served with. He has a typical response when asked, "What was it like to serve in the army?"

"I liked it! I got to experience Germany and learn about cool stuff every day!" he exclaims.

Mail call was once a week. One time, Tom received a check for $39.50 from home for his favorite blue '39 Plymouth coupe. He had to leave it behind for Calvin and Bob to sell for him. "I remember riding around in that car when I was just seven years old," Chris McKee recalls.

"Ginger was a knockout. She would dance around the kitchen at Grandma's house, helping with the dishes."

Grandma Ann was very traditional and conformity was in, but conformity was never in Ginger. Ann never missed an opportunity to make the routine comment to Ginger, with a sideways glance, "Hmm, so how long are you going to let your hair get?" Ginger would give a regal head toss and purr "When I'm sitting on it, I will pull it up in an elegant pin." The kids admired her, because no one talked back to Grandma, especially with such class.

Tom reading and writing
letters to Ginger.

Tom (in the middle) playing football with his buddies.

When one of the kids ran up and wrapped themselves around her leg, Ginger never missed the opportunity to bend down and tickle them, sending them running off, squealing. With a playful giggle and a swish of her full skirt, she would turn back to dancing to the music and drying the dishes as if they were fine china and the dish towel was a fine linen cloth.

Tom admired the Germans for being disciplined, efficient, and hardworking. "They were curious about us. When we walked down the street, they'd come out and walk with us to talk. Even with our different languages, we could manage. If a helicopter flew over, they would scatter and take cover. I felt bad for them, because they had been hammered for so long, but were hanging tough. When the *chuff-chuff-chuff* of the chopper would fade, the Germans would come back out, cautiously looking around, and all would have a laugh together. Talk about a good sense of humor! Don't worry, we are in this together," Tom would reassure them, and they would pat each other on the backs.

In the collection of letters Tom sent home are several pictures of historical crucifixes and beautiful cathedrals, a map, and lots of funny stories. The soldiers would sometimes get a three-day pass written in English and German. *"Thomas H. Russell is authorized to be absent for the purpose of visiting Germany, Switzerland, and Austria. I have been oriented by my commanding officer in military courtesy, discipline, and bearing, and I was inspected prior to departure."* Any downtime in the barracks was used for reading and Tom's favorite pastime, playing football!

The *Saturday Stars and Stripes* newspaper dated April 9, 1955 shows *"Super Weapons on Display."*

Pictured is an "Honest John" rocket, a 280mm cannon, and "Corporal," a guided missile. "I got to learn really cool stuff about rockets and missiles every day. We would have drills in case the Russians were coming. Our sergeant would slam the door really loud after he woke us up early every morning," Tom recalls with a chuckle.

Pirmasens, which is a German town near the border of France, had a club. Tom still has the trifold 2-½" x 3-½" membership card that lists a beer for twenty cents, homemade chili for a quarter, and ten-cent fries. The membership card listed just eight straight-to-the-point club rules. The club was closed on Fridays for private parties, otherwise open in the evenings. The Jazz floor show was every Saturday night. Those were the good ole days when people knew how to dress, how to act, not to "bring discredit to the military," and Coca-Cola was a nickel!

Finishing College

TU had taken some old army barracks and put up Quonset huts that at the time were right next to the campus (at the site of present-day Kiplinger Hall), called Veterans Village. The huts each held four families, and two of them faced each other, so eight families shared one tiny yard. Tom and Ginger lived there for two years. All he could afford for transportation was a motorcycle (okay, and he had a need for speed). He could walk to class and ride his cycle to his job.

He chose blue, of course, and Ginger rode the bus downtown to work. A love for riding motorcycles would eventually be passed on to four of his six kids. All three of his sons would end up flying planes too! His bike had such a loud rumble that he would coast it down the hill (a skill he had perfected as a kid with Calvin's bike) before firing it up.

* * *

Downtown, Ginger operated the telephone switch-board. It was a high-backed panel facing the operator with a keyboard and switches. The blue-and-red wires hanging out were used to connect the correct calls to the flashing lights. She wore professional, tailored clothes with matching gloves and handkerchiefs. She sat at her desk like Audrey Hepburn on a movie set instead of a farm girl from Bartlesville, OK, in a hand-sewn dress from scraps of material. She had acted in plays and had an affinity for the theatre.

"Do you want to know a naughty little trick, my darling?" she would inquire of an unsuspecting young lady in a mesmerizing manner. The girl would come forward like she was about to hear the juiciest secret. "Do you want to know how to shine on stage? The eye follows movement. A wise actress uses her props creatively. Always plan ahead what you are going to do with your hands. If you're holding

Ginger acting in a play.

Stylish Ginger ready to go

a fan, give it a subtle wave toward your face. The gentle breeze will also keep your makeup fresh under the bright lights," she would whisper.

Donna Funk once asked her aunt Ginger, "Why are the buttons of your dress in the front? I thought they were supposed to go in the back."

"A lady wears her buttons, my love. The buttons don't wear her." Ginger winked and smiled.

There was a flower shop underneath her office that would discard cut flowers all over the ground while preparing arrangements. On her way in to work, Ginger would search for the perfect one in the same color of her outfit that day. She always had a single, fresh, pretty flower proudly displayed on her desk. Fall time was her favorite. You would find her twirling the most perfect, interesting, brightly colored red-orange leaf in her delicate fingers. "Look at that. Isn't it perfect?" she'd say as she held it up to admire. "It just floated to the ground and gently landed like a bird." She would hold her leaf and sway side to side, watching it glisten in the sunlight and humming a melody. That leaf would soon be resting on her windowsill.

* * *

TU turned out to be more than a just place to earn a degree. For Tom, it was an institution with lifelong benefits. The proximity of their hut was convenient for class. When his chemical engineering instructor Paul Buthod would write equations on the board, Tom would see a gas plant in his head. "That's what made him such an effective teacher. He gave me all the tools I needed to get my first job." Later in his career, Tom would call on Paul Buthod for help solving gas-processing problems, as well as for suggesting prime candidates for Tom's company. Tom was listed in the 1956 edition of *Who's Who in American Universities & Colleges.*

Son, no one refuses a transfer to Dallas.

– Tom's boss

Chapter 4

BIG CITY, JIM, & HOUSE

First Job

After graduating *cum laude* from TU in May of 1957, his B.S. degree in Chemical Engineering in hand, Tom and Ginger packed up their modest possessions and their one-year-old baby. Ginger recalled, "Us and everything we had fit into one car." They headed to Spivey, Kansas, for Tom's first job as an engineer with a family and a broom handle sticking out the window. On their grand exit out of T-Town into the big world, they promptly broke down and were stranded on the side of the road in the heat of the summer. "We will be just fine. Besides, I have a broom for protection," Ginger joked. Tom had to walk to a phone to call his sister Pat for assistance. They

eventually made it to Magnolia Petroleum Company
in Kansas.

Tom was earning a decent salary and enjoying quail
hunting on the weekends. He was comfortable. He had his
first company car, a two-door Chevy Impala. One day his
boss called him in and offered him a transfer to their Dallas
office, which Tom declined. His boss solemnly got up, walked
over, shut the door, and then turned to Tom and said words
he will never forget. "Son, nobody refuses a transfer to Dallas."

Tom chuckles as he recalls, "Everyone wanted to go
work for Bruner Barnes. He was brilliant." There wouldn't
be a company car waiting—he would have to ride the bus
and work his way up—but it was a flattering promotion
his boss wasn't going to let him miss. Without hesitation,
Ginger packed up, and off to the big city of Dallas they went.

* * *

The Texas oil boom of the twentieth century,
sometimes called the Gusher Age, began a period of
dramatic change and economic growth when a petroleum
reserve (the strike at Spindletop) was discovered at a
salt dome near Beaumont. Salt domes can deform the

overlaying rock, trapping oil and natural gas. Texas quickly became one of the leading oil-producing states (100,000 barrels of oil per day), along with Oklahoma and California, surpassing the Soviet Union as the top producer of petroleum. The record overabundance of supply dropped the price to a record low of three cents per barrel, less than the price of water in some areas.

A usual day at work would change with a phone call from W. A. Moncrief, Jr., or "Tex." "I have a reservation for you at a hotel in Arkansas," his voice would grumble matter-of-factly.

"I'm on my way," Tom would answer.

While working for Barnes and Click in Ft. Worth, Tex would sometimes hire Tom to test gas wells. Once he checked into his hotel, he would receive the next assignment. "He was a smart, no-bull kind of guy," Tom remarks. "It was always exciting to be dispatched on his missions, and he knew I would go and deliver. That's how we worked."

Times were different back then. Safety regulations have come a long way over time. Tom recalls, "One day Jim Hamilton came into the doghouse in Texas looking like he had been in a windstorm." Jim had opened a valve into a high-pressure line, which blew high-pressure gas right in his face, but he just went on with what he was doing. Nowadays you have to wear safety gear and follow various procedures.

Most contracts specified that wells had to be in production on a certain day or the producer had to pay a penalty. Tom recalls, "A guy would come into the doghouse and say you had to be tied into that pipeline one week from now." Tom could see the ditching machine over the hill laying the pipeline, knowing they were about two to three weeks out. There was always pressure to work harder and finish jobs sooner. Tom enjoyed his work but had a pipe dream to build! He was eager to get into the construction part, but how?

Cowboy Club

While working in Dallas, Tom joined his favorite football team's club. The Dallas Cowboys would host a monthly lunch, and a featured player would be there for a meet-and-greet. The team had formed in 1960 with Tom Landry as the first coach. Tom never missed his luncheon and never missed a game. The Thanksgiving Day game was a tradition. He has been with his team from the beginning and is a lifelong fan. He would later name the family dog Star after his favorite quarterback, Roger Staubach.

He watched every presidential debate as well. The black-and-white TV had become the primary medium for influencing public opinion. Making a decent salary now, he and Ginger were able to score one for about $100.

Designing Belle Creek & Big Jim

"Wildcatter" Sam Gary discovered eight oil fields while drilling in the mountains of Montana in June 1967. They needed a design for a processing plant, took a shot, and called Tom at Barnes & Click, Inc. "So, do you think you could do it?" Sam Gary's right-hand man, Turner Smith, inquired.

Never one to back down from a challenge and knowing this was his lucky chance to build, Tom answered, "You bet!" and got right to work on the design. He teamed up with Jim Dorough, who ran the shop they used at Bering Gas Company. Jim had never graduated college and, without a degree, he had worked his way up every day. This was the beginning of not only a great working relationship, but also a friendship that lasted for the next thirty-five years until Jim's passing.

Once the plant is assembled in the field, starting it up takes about two weeks. Going "on stream" in November in the mountains of Montana can get cold, down to -40° F. Everyone else went home at night, but Jim and Tom had the same work ethic; they weren't going anywhere. They slept at the plant, staying with their project.

Imagine a man every bit of 6' and 250 lbs. trying to balance and get comfy in a wheelbarrow. Jim tried resting his legs on the handles, hanging them down, many different positions. "I was cracking up, watching this go on," Tom recalls. "He kept getting up and moving his wheelbarrow a little closer to the heater, then he would climb back in for another test run. It was like watching a guy teetering on a raft, just waiting to see a flip and hear a splash." His nickname of Big Jim was born, and so was their lifelong partnership. "We never wrote anything down. We didn't need to. We had each other's backs. Our trust was rock solid," says Tom.

"It's so exciting to fire up a gas plant!" Tom exclaims. "You get one area of the plant going, then go the next, and so on. You stand back and look up at this massive structure doing this incredible thing." The plant processed 13.5 MMcfd from four hundred wells. That's a technical term meaning "million standard cubic feet per day," a unit of measurement for gases processed in the U.S. "It makes a super high-pitched scream when the valves are first opened. It's LOUD. That's a lot of pressure!"

As the plant was absorbing the valuable hydrocarbons in the gas from the ground, Tom was absorbing a realization. "I designed this!" This was what he wanted to do, he was sure of it. "Let's go back to Tulsa. I want to build," Tom informed Ginger.

"You got it!" she replied.

Open House Goes Haywire

Balloons were swaying in the gentle breeze, and the smell of fresh-baked bread wafted through the humble little house for sale in Dallas. The place had been cleaned from top to bottom (not an easy task with four kids running around). It was spiffed up as much as possible.

At 12:30 p.m., Ginger stepped out on the porch and looked around. "Why isn't anyone coming to our open house?" Tom was at work as usual, but it was eerily quiet. No one was prepared for the complete chaos about to erupt like a volcano.

"Ahhh! Oh no! This isn't happening! I can't believe it!" Neighbors screamed and cried out as they ran up the streets and into their homes to turn on their TVs. Cars came screeching into their drives, people jumping out, leaving their doors open, spilling their belongings, leaving a trail of debris. "President Kennedy has been shot!" someone wailed.

Oswald didn't hate Kennedy. He hated what he stood for, and he hated America, and he wasn't the only one. He had remarked to a Marine that "the best religion is communism."

During the 1960 West Virginia Primary, senator John F. Kennedy addressed the issue head on in a speech before the American Society of Newspaper Editors:

> *Are we going to admit to the world that a Jew can be elected Mayor of Dublin, a Protestant can be chosen Foreign Minister of France, a Muslim can be elected to the Israeli Parliament—but a Catholic cannot be President of the United States? Are we going to admit*

to the world—worse still, are we going to admit to ourselves—that one-third of the American people is forever barred from the White House?

A group of one hundred and fifty Protestant ministers met in Washington and demanded that Kennedy could not remain independent of their control. They demanded he repudiate his beliefs immediately! Instead, Senator Kennedy received a standing ovation and nearly universal praise from the press for his eloquent performance addressing the Greater Houston Ministerial Association. After his presidential inauguration, he stated, "I think we have buried the religion issue once and for all." It turned out he was wrong.

Second Open House Goes Haywire

When things seemingly calmed down a bit, deadlines were once again pressing, and people were somberly trying to get back to work and carry on with President Johnson at the helm. Ginger had chores to do and a family to move. She blew up some more balloons and baked another loaf of sweet-smelling fresh bread. Modest belongings were packed away and ready to go as soon as they could sell the house, otherwise they would not have the means to relocate. Ginger emerged onto her porch, looked around, and wondered why no one was showing up to the second open house. The sign was out, but the streets were empty.

No one was prepared for the aftershock and "absolute panic" about to ensue. While being escorted from the basement of the police station to the courthouse, one of Kennedy's murderers, Oswald had been shot by Jack Ruby on live TV! People were again glued to their TVs, their only source of information in this evolving American tragedy.

BACK IN TULSA AND THE BIG HOUSE

In 1969 Neil Armstrong and Buzz Aldrin became the first men to land on the moon. Landing back in Tulsa, Tom was getting a crash course in the corporate world. He was now building process heaters for Econotherm. Tom convinced Big Jim to move his family to Tulsa and run the shop there. "He knew how to run a shop," Tom says with certainty. At the office, the Econotherm Company was struggling financially. Tom watched helplessly as the owners made terrible decisions and sold jobs to customers without knowing their costs.

* * *

"Who keeps beating up Glenn?" Tom asked at the dinner table. Glenn was about six years old at the time. Both Glenn and Matt's heads were shaved per Tom's military-style preference. It was the third time he had shown up with his swollen eyes cast down and his face mangled. Being the new kid in town wasn't in style, neither was not having long hair in the '60s.

"A bully," Jenny said in between bites of her casserole.

"The big kid a few houses down," Matt added as he chewed.

The table got quiet, and the mood was solemn. Moving to a new place wasn't an easy transition for the kids. With limited funds and only one car, the kids had to ride the bus to public school. Hand-me-down, tattered clothes and poverty wasn't in style either.

Tom looked at Ginger with a low, calm but stern tone, "Start sending Russells until the job gets done" he said. Ginger responded with a nod.

"You are no one's punching bag, son," Tom said as he got up from the table. "I have to go back to the office."

Ginger knew she had to send her "babies" into battle. It was the only way they would learn to defend themselves, and others—to stand up for what was right.

Stand for What Is Right at 46″ Tall

Glenn shuffled up to the neighbor's door. The bell chimed inside. When the door opened, there stood a kid twice Glenn's size, looking down at him as if he were crazy for showing up there like that. **POW!** Glenn gave it all he had and punched the bully in the stomach! The bully was momentarily stunned but then started to swell up like the Hulk. Glenn spun around, and the chase was on! He had some practice with his siblings, but this was a serious situation.

He booked it across the front yard as fast as his legs could go. Just as he felt the bully reach for his collar and thought, *This might be it,* he felt his body lift off and go airborne as he leaped over the ditch. Guess who was lying in wait inside the curve of the ditch? Jenny jumped up, and

Matt jumped out from behind a tree. That was the last time they were bullied in their new neighborhood.

FIRED

During the usual monthly committee meeting at Econotherm about how each department was going to cut costs, try to save money, and avoid an inevitable bankruptcy, Tom sat and listened as the self-preserving managers around the room offered ideas. "I will fire two secretaries." "I will sell one company car." "We will all bring our own coffee mugs from home." "If it's yellow, let it mellow."

Tom rose from his chair and said, "I will fire myself."

"What? You can't do that!" the baffled management exclaimed.

"My salary is twenty percent of the debt, and I will never ask anyone to endure what I am not willing to endure myself." Tom turned and walked out the door, determined to own his own small business that operated with a big heart.

Big Jim picked up his wheelbarrow and followed Tom out the door. Jim started Mohawk Steel.

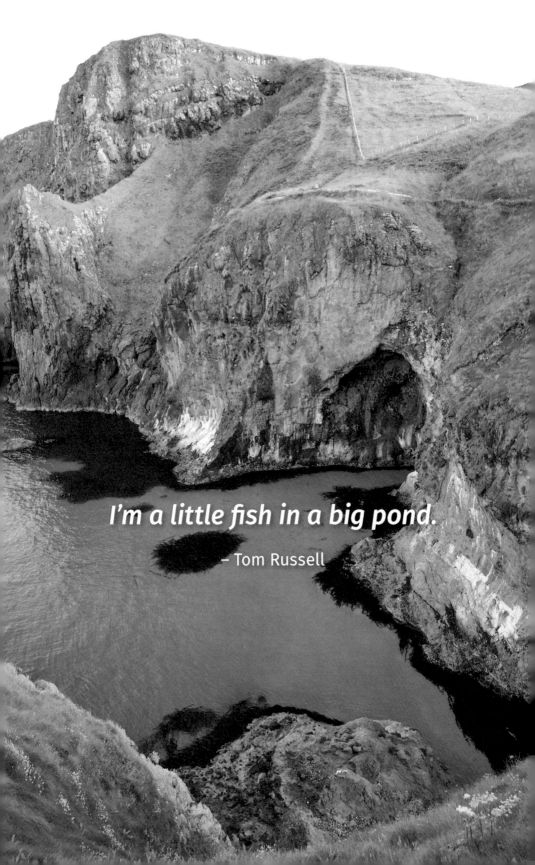

I'm a little fish in a big pond.

– Tom Russell

Chapter 5

THE T.H. RUSSELL COMPANY

T.H. Russell Company, 1971–2000

Tom was armed with fifteen years of experience and many valuable contacts. His past experience had focused on processing for the first three years, four years of equipment manufacture and installation, two years of plant construction, and the last six had been consulting on all of the above. He realized he had experience in all phases of the gas plant business. Why not provide customers with all the phases under one roof? A total program, he thought. T.H. was taking a big personal and professional risk to strike out on his own with five kids and a pregnant wife.

He had put in many extra hours on plant start-ups and maintenance shut downs. He was registered in Texas, Oklahoma, and later Colorado. All he lacked was the funds. T.H. went to the banks but was denied a loan. There wasn't enough collateral, meaning he didn't own anything to put up for a loan. He remembered his neighbor down the street, George Kaiser. The boys mowed his lawn, and until now he and George had just made small talk. That was about to change.

APPLYING FOR A LOAN

T.H. stood on Mr. Kaiser's porch a virtual stranger. Kaiser's parents were Jewish and had escaped Nazi Germany, settling in Oklahoma. He was known to work seventy hours a week and avoided the spotlight. He had a little white sign in his yard that said, "Kaiser-Francis Oil Co." He also owned a bank. "I'm a little fish in a big pond," T.H. said when the business mogul opened his door.

Kaiser intuitively knew the quality of the man who had the bravery to show up on his doorstep. He also knew the challenges one faced when starting

T.H. starting his business in 1972.

a business. Kaiser gave T.H. the loan he needed to feed his family and get going on the company. Once strangers but now acquaintances, they would see each other again when T.H. donated to Kaiser's Gathering Place Park on Riverside.

Once T.H. was ready to design and build gas plants, Ginger typed his brochure:

T.H. Russell Co.
Specializing in
Design, Evaluation, and Construction
of
Natural Gas and Gas Liquid Facilities
Tulsa, OK

His services were listed as field test and supervision at $16 an hour, designing at $20 an hour, and $25 a court appearance. Considerable time was spent driving around, making calls, and getting the word out. He definitely knew he wanted his plants to be low-cost, well-designed and modular! Modular construction was a new idea in those days. He was certain how he wanted things to run financially after working for a company he'd watched go bankrupt. No doubt he knew how he wanted people treated. He hoped his kids would join his passion some day, after they "learned their mistakes on someone else's money," just like he had. He had integrity and innovation in mind…not dollar signs, and not "shoo-ins."

Working Mom

In typical ladylike style, Ginger had complete confidence in her husband. In addition to running the home, she assisted T.H. with running his new business. "You never call anyone before 8am or after 5pm. When Dad's home from work, that's family time. A man doesn't need to be told how to do his job, and a woman doesn't need to be told how to run her home," she would advise the children. She encouraged her husband and took care of their six children. They sure don't make them like that anymore. She made being a housewife look so glamorous and powerful. She made womanhood wonderful. T.H. had to work 24/7 and was willing to answer that phone if it would only please just ring.

Off-limits were any demands from the children until after Dad had eaten his dinner, even if that was a plate wrapped in foil waiting on the table long after everyone else had swooped in like ravenous buzzards and already flown off. With a slow and steady puff of her cigarette, Ginger would say, "Careful kids, he is going to make it someday, but he isn't happy when he is hungry, so let him eat." Out of little, eager, hungry mouths when the family gathered around the table had better come phrases like "How was work today?" Never, "I want... I need... When are we going to... When are you going to get me...?"

* * *

During long road trips, Ginger would wrap his sandwich with the paper around the bottom of it to protect any spillage onto his pants (she and Chick-fil-A know how it's done), quietly place a napkin on his leg, then ask him a question about work. He would start chattering away about gas plants while the kids grew weary of elbowing each other and nodded off.

After his sandwich, she would hand him his hand-gripper exercise device or his Dictaphone. "You can always be doing something productive," he would say. Ginger, the copilot, had better be ready at a moment's notice to retrieve his map from the glove box and strategically fold it to show the state they were currently in. "You were just seeing if the map was right, because I knew you were," she would coo.

A Good Name Is a Good Man

T.H. knew that many companies had generic names the owner and employees could hide behind. Instead, he welcomed the accountability that came with having his name associated with the work he did. With his innovation and integrity, he wanted to make sure he had a company and a reputation that he could be proud of. Part of T.H.'s confidence came from his understanding that the chance for success for honest men willing to work hard was much greater in the United States of America than in any other part of the world. Patriotic to the bone, he believed that the streets really were paved with gold. He knew we hadn't come all this way to claim victimhood.

The first entries listed in T.H.'s expense journal, dated 12-31-71, are for the basic necessities of a home

office: a typewriter for $130, a $121 desk, a bookcase/
file cabinet for $50, and a '69 Pontiac financed through
the bank with $71.41 payments due monthly. He
joined the Petroleum Club so he and Ginger could meet
important contacts.

* * *

It wasn't easy to find a babysitter, since the kids were
so rowdy. No one ever came back twice to watch the kids.

Next-door neighbor Celia came a few times and let
Mandy drive her Trans Am! "How fast can I go?" Mandy
would ask.

"Till it scares ya," Celia would calmly say.

Karen Moran was Ginger's niece and also watched
the kids, and if she hadn't been related, I'm sure we never
would have seen her again either.

* * *

With some minimal earnings doing consulting work,
finances were tight, and T.H. borrowed money from
everyone he could. He even cleaned out what little money
had been put away in the kids' savings accounts. "I will

pay you back with interest," he promised the kids. He kept his promises. The thirty-eight-year-old entrepreneur worked off a little desk and telephone in the bedroom of their house. Ginger was his "secretary," his only "employee" at the time. He always kept an ink pen in the pocket of his shirt. She got good at salvaging his only collared shirt when it again sported a big ink stain after the wash.

Job #101

T.H. was driving to any town he had a contact in, trying to get business. He needed work, and the phone wasn't ringing. On New Year's Eve 1971, he drove twelve long hours back from West Texas. Despite all the celebrations going on, all T.H. had on his mind for the next year was finding ways to earn a living and feed his family. He crawled into bed in the middle of the night, exhausted and hoping for a miracle, or at least some renewed energy to be able to keep going.

T.H. was usually up at the crack of dawn with the news blaring on the TV in the background, grapefruit peelings on the counter beside a glass containing remnants of instant chocolate breakfast mix. But this particular morning he was still asleep at eight o'clock. This was "sleeping in" for him.

Ginger poked her head in the dark room. "There's someone on the phone for you."

T.H. managed to rouse enough to sit on the side of the bed and pick up the line. He heard a deep, gruff voice on the other end. "If you think you're going to make it out on your own, you have to get your tail out of bed in the morning!" It was Jimmy L. Davis with Adobe Oil Co. in Midland, TX, whom T.H. had visited during one of his rounds.

T.H. jumped up, went to his desk, and produced a hand-drawn flow diagram of a standard refrigeration plant with a pencil on a piece of paper. After J.L. was able to look it over, along with a quote, he called T.H. back.

"Looks fine. The job is yours."

T.H. Russell Co. was off and running!

T.H. strategically named it Job #101, not simply #1, to make it look like he had a hundred other jobs under the belt. He used Big Jim's shop at Mohawk for the construction. It was a New Year miracle. T.H. Russell Company had its very first job!

Everyone was slow paying in those days. Ginger typed the statement for him. At the bottom of the $4,500 invoice, T.H. wrote, *"Can you pay this a little quicker, please?"*

J.L. not only admired the quality of the work, he was impressed by the assertiveness of the young boss he had taken a chance on to give this important job. This was the springboard for word to get around and hopefully more jobs to come in!

JOBS #102-105

As with any business startup, the first few years are critical, and T.H. was within days of having to close his doors. He was soon going to have to find work elsewhere, anywhere. The Christmas decorations were still up. T.H. managed to wake up every morning with a new "can-do attitude."

For Job #102, he swallowed his pride and knocked on the door of his former employer, Econotherm, on January 4, 1972. He was able to get a project installing one of their heaters. This yielded a much-needed income of $1,514.53.

It was getting to the end of the month when Wenco gave him Job #103 for half as much to solve a problem with the operation of a plant. At the end of February, T.H. reviewed plant operations for N.C. Ginther, Job #104. March brought the company Job #105. Calvert Exploration hired him to calculate compressor sizes for some of their wells. Work was picking up slowly but surely. T.H. had figured out early in life to make good use of any downtime, always stay positive, and continue onward with courage.

It was springtime in April, so he took the boys camping. While collecting some of the Funk cousins for the trip, what seemed like a typical day at the Funk house changed with the ring of a telephone. "A man named Mr. Turner Smith is looking for T.H.," Ginger told Aunt Eileen. When the camping crew arrived and got the message, he immediately called her back using his sister's phone. "Something about needing a plant moved from Montana to Utah and wondering if you could do it," Ginger relayed. The area had dried up of gas reserves. T.H. knew that plant well. After all, he had designed it.

Job #106 "Gary," Moving the Bell Creek Plant

A year after T.H. started his new business, he got his first really big job and his first big break! This was also a tall order. It would require renting cranes, a crew, huge flatbed trucks, and paying workers, all of which required funds he didn't have. "I sure can," he told the customer. Turkeys still only have two drumsticks, but the Russell family was able to pass a platter of meat around the table because of this job.

"What did you do, Dad? How did you do it?" the kids would later ask.

"I rolled up my sleeves and got to work!" T.H. remembers. "I had to tell people, 'I will pay you what I can when I can, with interest.'" T.H. is a man of his word, and anyone who dealt with him knew it.

When someone questioned or criticized him, he would calmly answer, "I don't have to defend myself to you. I will just keep doing what I do every day, and that will speak for itself." It makes no difference to T.H where you came from or if you're an expert. The only thing that matters to him is "Are you a **good hand**?" He believes everyone has the potential to be a good hand if they want to. "We can all find things to worry about…or we can get up and get going."

He knew just whom to call: his best friend. Big Jim was immediately on board, helping T.H. figure out how they were going to get the job done. Failure was not an option.

* * *

T.H. took five-year-old Jenny with him to Montana to scope out the work ahead. Jenny had one desire. "Can I ride a horse? Please, please, please!" The excited little girl jumped up and down.

The gruff ole cowboy locked eyes with Tom, but Jenny wasn't letting up. The cowboy looked down at Jenny. "No, hon." They all turned to walk in the direction of the job site.

"Please!" Jenny pleaded.

The cowboy stopped and decided to level with the Okies. "She would die out there, sir. There are rattlesnakes, mountain lions, no fences…. It's not a good idea."

They resumed walking, looking around at the vast wilderness that stretched as far as the eye could see.

* * *

T.H. decided to rent an office and move his business out of the bedroom on the first of May. He found a spot available at Fike's strip at 51st and Lewis for $60 a month, which later became Parkhill's liquor store.

Job #107 came from George Kaiser for the design of a gas well delivery system. Jobs #108-110 were plant designs for McDaniel, Gary, and BSB. Job #111 was for lawsuit assistance for Rayon & Smith. Those are the last entries in T.H.'s logbook. The rest is history and is recorded here to the best of his kids' recollection.

Tempting Proposal

A few years later, a potential customer approached T.H., needing a processing plant to clean up the incoming gas. "If you give me a *silent* extra 25% profit, if you know what I mean, I'll give you this job," he whispered. "This will put you in business!" This was a very tempting offer and much-needed income, but T.H. had a gut feeling that this wasn't how business was supposed to go…if you wanted to have honest dealings.

Calvin visited T.H. to walk him through the conclusion he knew he would arrive at. They sat in lounge chairs with a little Irish whiskey on the rocks and cigars. (The word whiskey comes from the Irish translation "water of life." It was once the most popular spirit in the world until, you guessed it, after the 1900s.) Kids were running all around the house, under Ginger's protective eyes, but not in the living room where the men were talking.

"I could do this job, my work would be quality, it would be profitable, and I would have more say when I got it up and going," T.H. pondered.

With a little sip and a puff of his cigar, Calvin leaned his head back. "Is this the kind of person you want to do business with?" he posed.

"No, it isn't," T.H. admitted to his mentor and himself.

"Don't deal with crooks. It isn't worth the money or your reputation," Calvin confirmed.

It turned out to be a crooked offer from a crooked guy. He was trying to get T.H. in on the deal as a contractor, where he would have hidden a piece of it. It was an underhanded deal and another important lesson learned.

My brothers, consider it a great joy when trials of many kinds come upon you, for you well know that the testing of your faith produces perseverance, and perseverance must complete its work so that you will become fully developed, complete, not deficient in any way. James 1:2-4.

Modularization

Usually how the gas business worked was that the customer came to a gas plant builder with the "gas analysis" of an area they had obtained the rights to lease. The builder would design a plant based on the gas analysis, so the plants were custom-built to be permanent to that specific area. Wanting to tap into the source immediately to start selling it, the company would "stick build" the gas plants on the land right away. This means all the parts and pieces of a plant were brought to the site, and often consideration wasn't given to the gas analysis changing as more wells were drilled. Also, taking gas from the wells changed the gas. The lighter hydrocarbons (ethane) usually come first, and then years later you start getting lesser quality gas, then just dirty contaminated liquids. Then the plant and area dried up and was abandoned. All the equipment is wasted.

T.H. developed his system of what he believed was the perfect process, which was the reverse of how it had been done up till now. The new concept was revolutionary, and modular plants became standard for T.H. Russell Company. The design time is done in the office, the construction in the nearby shop, and then the "skid-mounted" sections are moved and connected out in the field (the customer's lot). Most of the work is done in the shop.

This process was faster and simpler than sending the whole crew out on location away from home, working in the rain and snow, often in very remote locations, designing as you went, paying overtime, renting expensive cranes for long periods, and custom-building a permanent, limited-lifetime plant. T.H. Russell Company was ahead of the game because they weren't "custom-built"…they were already built, ready to go.

Skid Mounting

T.H. gained insight from designing and then moving the Bell Creek plant on ways to do his skid-mounting technique. It wasn't a completely new concept (the military used a form of it), but his company would perfect it. T.H. was eventually able to rent some land off of Highway 11 for construction. It was next to Mohawk Steel. It was here that T.H. began building skids. A skid is a steel frame supporting various tanks, pumps, heat exchanges, piping and valves, and electrical controls. Skids are then loaded onto large flat trucks and transported to the jobsite. These same skids can be moved years later to a new jobsite much easier than a stick-built plant.

Natural Gas

Also called fossil gas, natural gas is a breakdown of layers of decomposing plant and animal matter (cow poop) exposed to intense heat and pressure in the deep underground rock formations over millions of years. The "nonrenewable" energy is stored in the form of chemical

103

A photographic moment for an Irish engineer to be driving by and see a rainbow over a plant.

bonds in the hydrocarbons. Light hydrocarbons include methane (natural gas), nitrogen, propane (farm fuel), and butane (for BIC lighters). Then there are heavier hydrocarbons, all the way to lubricating oil. It is often mixed with nitrogen, carbon dioxide, water, sulfur, and even helium.

Fracking is when millions of gallons of water and sand are injected at high pressure into horizontal wells to crack open shale rock and release natural gas. We will explore more on that subject later. Shale is a fragile rock formed from clay and can be split easily in between slabs. It is found where water has deposited sediments that have become compacted into a weak rock. Clay is used for ceramics.

Renewable energy refers to wind, water, and solar power and is a different ball game. Oil and gas are normally found together. T.H. Russell Company built gas plants, which processed the lighter hydrocarbons for the most part, although occasionally they would build plants for the heavier stuff.

North America and Europe are the major consumers of natural gas. The United States is the largest producer. Most natural gas is burned for fuel. It burns cleaner than other fuels, such as oil or coal. About 35% of the natural gas consumed in the U.S. is used for electric power, 34% for industrial use, 17% for residential use, 12% for commercial use, and 3% for transportation.

Gasoline, diesel, and jet fuel are processed differently. They are made from crude oil (the heavier stuff) pumped out of the ground (almost 80% domestically). It is formed largely from the breakdown of algae and zooplankton in the ocean. This is what companies like Shell, Chevron, ExxonMobil, and others are about.

The United States alone needs about 30 trillion cubic feet of natural gas to keep going. Five states are the highest producers: Texas, California, Louisiana, Florida, then lastly Pennsylvania. It is a major source of electricity generation when used with gas and steam turbines. It is used residentially for gas ranges, ovens, clothes dryers, furnaces, water heaters, and even air conditioners.

GAS PROCESSING

The first modern chemist was Robert Boyle from Lismore, County Waterford, in Ireland, the same county that T.H.'s lineage is from. In 1616 Boyle published what is considered to be a masterpiece of scientific literature. He is credited with Boyle's Law, discovering that the volume of gas decreases with increasing pressure and vice versa. He is known as a seventeenth-century pioneer of modern chemistry. T.H. Russell is known as a twentieth-century pioneer of gas processing after perfecting his craft for forty-one years.

Natural gas processing means taking "raw" gas out of the ground, cleaning it by separating out impurities and water, then separating the hydrocarbons from each other (methane, propane, butane, etc.). A fully operational plant delivers pipeline-quality dry natural gas that can be used as fuel by residential, commercial, and industrial consumers.

TORNADO IN DALLAS

T.H. never stopped pounding the pavement and was eventually able to rent a bigger office at 49th and Skelly and hire some other engineers. The company had its first employees. One of them was Don Purcell. One day T.H. and Don Purcell heard of a storm brewing in Dallas. While on a trip to a jobsite near Dallas, they stopped at a roadside café for coffee. There was a chalkboard on the wall listing specials. A waitress walked up to it, erased the specials, and started writing highway closures. One by one, all the main accesses were closing. A fierce Midwest summer storm was raging.

They took the back roads and finally arrived at the plant, which was now a ghost town, with the strong winds blowing and rain hammering down. They slept in the car at the plant that night. If anything was going to happen, it was going to happen to them while everyone else was home with their families.

* * *

Hub Ferrell, a mechanical engineer, joined T.H. in 1975. Hub was an excellent engineer who solved many of the challenging problems that T.H. Russell Company faced. By this time, they had fancier brochures with color pictures. It featured pouring concrete in freezing snowy weather, a 390,000-gallon product storage unit, and a plant for Getty that produced ten tons of sulfur per day. Also featured was their shop used for fabrication and skid assembly. It listed over twenty-five impressive clients and then asked, "May we add your name to our list of satisfied clients?"

THE COMPANY'S FIRST SHOP

The shop employees had been working outside in the elements with no amenities anywhere around. T.H. showed up one day and saw a different kind of construction going on. There were piles of lumber, metal siding, hardware, and

The second shop was steel framed.

men he didn't recognize busy with the materials. "What's going here?" he inquired.

"We are building a shop for a Mr. Russell."

"I'm Mr. Russell," T.H. informed them. The structure was a pole barn that would surely provide shelter. "Who ordered this?"

One of the busy workers replied, "Jim Durough said you needed a shop put in here at this location."

What a nice gift, what a nice friend, what a nice guy! No paperwork needed. That was how they operated.

Financial Fit

Soon Mike Pollard joined the new company as Chief Financial Officer. "I want to know every single month how much we have in these jobs, and how much it's going to take to finish them," T.H. explained, outlining his expectations. He had learned from watching other companies that financial trouble started with the bidding at the very beginning. Unrealistic low bids were submitted to the customer. Then costs shifted, sometimes a little, more often a lot. They wouldn't know what they had in a job until they shipped it. Cost wouldn't be added up until after, and it would be a loss. To compensate, they would sell more jobs at a loss, then lay off experienced people. T.H.'s new accountant was on board with keeping a close eye on costs, planning for the shifts and the ups and downs, and absolutely avoiding layoffs if possible.

T.H. knew what it was like to live on the chopping block. He recalls, "The big guys would come into town and have a meeting, and we would all have to sit, wait, and wonder who was going to go. We all had families to feed, children, pregnant wives. It wasn't easy to find work elsewhere once you had been kicked out. It was always so stressful and sad to see your friends go, or do the walk of shame with your little box." He vowed he wouldn't treat his people that way. "That's not the way to do business," he decided.

Administrative Assistant

Do you know anyone who can type 110 words per minute, answer the phone with her toes, and leap tall buildings in a single bound? Johnnie Dubler can. A few days after she came to work for him, T.H. scanned one of the letters she had typed, handed it back to her, and said, "Look here, you left off an S." He pointed to the spot. "I'm only interested in top quality around here."

Ginger was patrolling the office space and making sure everyone was settling in and had everything they needed. "Johnnie is sharp. Wouldn't you be happy to focus on what you would rather be doing?" she suggested to T.H.

Then she approached Johnnie. "Do you want to know how to keep him happy? Make sure he is fed. He will work right through a tornado and not even eat," she advised the new assistant.

The next day T.H. arrived bright and early to find a doughnut sitting on his desk. Underneath it was a note from Johnnie:

Attention T.H.

SSSSSSSSSSSSSSSSSSSSSSSSSSS
SSSSSSSSSSSSSSSSSSSSSSSSSSS
SSSSSSSSSSSSSSSSSSSSSSSSSSS
SSSSSSSSSSSSSSSSSSSSSSSSSSS
SSSSSSSSSSSSSSSSSSSSSSSSSSS

Sincerely, Johnnie

He busted out laughing and knew they were going to be a perfect match. She wasn't going to take any grief from him and could most definitely produce only top quality. She had stayed all night to complete everything he needed, with all T's crossed and I's dotted, and all the S's he could stand with a doughnut on top. It wasn't long before T.H. entrusted her with the authority to sign his checks and much more.

112

Along with T.H.'s sense of humor came a strong sense of the seriousness of customer satisfaction. Around Christmas, T.H. called one of his engineers to inform him there was a problem at a plant in Midland, TX, and would he please take care of it?

"Do I need to remind you that it is a holiday and I have a family?" the engineer scoffed at him.

Johnnie heard her boss say, "Do I have to remind you that you installed pumps which aren't working?" T.H. made sure his customers were taken care of 24/7/365.

GPA Fashion Show

Once T.H.'s company had a functioning office and staff, Ginger was freed up to focus on more important things… like fashion! Not having the funds for fancy clothes never stopped that farm girl before, and it wasn't about to now. For a formal GPA (Gas Processing Association) party, Ginger got out her bathrobe and spiffed it up. She pinned a beautiful jeweled brooch to its lapel. It was a cherished heirloom from her redheaded mother, Genevieve "Mama used to dance the cha cha when women weren't supposed to dance the cha cha," she said, beaming as she twirled the terry cloth robe from side to side in the mirror.

"You are *not* going to wear that robe to this fancy party, are you, Mom?" the kids cried out, rolling on the floor with their sticky hands covering their faces in horror.

Ginger struck a pose with her hand on her hip and bent down to caress her children's cheeks. "I'm going to walk into that room with my head held high in my fancy evening gown, my darlings," she explained.

"Well, maybe you shouldn't smoke, then," Mandy offered.

"Why?" Ginger inquired.

"Because it's bad for you, and I heard secondhand smoke is bad for me!"

Ginger knelt down, smiled, and motioned for Mandy to come closer. Ginger leaned forward and whispered, "If I didn't smoke, sweetheart, I would have strangled you by now." And she winked.

Ginger saved up and planned to attend a future convention in a beautiful evening gown. "I'm going to show them I look just as good in a gown as I do in my bathrobe!" She planned and saved until the moment arrived. Her hair was immaculate, and her makeup was "made for the movies." She practiced her elegant moves in her high-heeled shoes.

Looking out the hotel window, she saw a lot of people moving about wearing plaid shirts, cowboy hats, and cowboy boots. "There must be a rodeo in town," she remarked. When it was time for their grand entrance into the event, she slipped into her matching gloves and picked up her clutch. She draped her wrap around her shoulders and was ready to go. When she heard the beep of the elevator, she was poised and ready to emerge…into the hoedown-themed party. That's right, the dress code had a western motif. Oops!

Speaking of Fashion

T.H. got an expense report back from one of his guys, Jim Powers, nicknamed "Cajun," whom he had sent out to meet with customers. "What is all this shopping stuff? I sent you down there to do a job, not go shopping," he annoyingly questioned.

"Well, Chief, you sent me down there in a go-to-hell hat and seersucker suit. I did do the job…and I had to dress the part to do it right!"

With that, T.H. burst out laughing. "Okay, you got me there, but next time dress yourself before you go."

* * *

In 1981 T.H. hired an electrical engineer, Craig Wentworth. He showed up for his first day in a coat and tie. T.H., in his jeans and boots, paraded Craig from office to office. "Look how nice he looks. Why don't you all dress like him?" he would say. Craig quickly lost his coat and tie and settled right in to the office after the initiation parade.

"You could stand to spiff yourself up," Big Jim joked to his buddy one day. A box soon arrived to "the big house" (a nickname for T.H. and Ginger's house) containing a Rolex watch. Big Jim knew T.H. would never spend money on something like that and wanted to treat him.

TURKEYS AND CALENDARS

T.H. always made sure that Mr. Turner Smith (from Job #106, moving the Bell Creek plant) was on the list for a

Christmas turkey. That job was a major turning point for his company. T.H. received a note from Mr. Smith one day, thanking him for his generosity but explaining that he hadn't bought a plant in a long time and that T.H. didn't need to feel obligated to keep sending him a turkey. The response says it all about how a salesman handles "no" and how a salesman should be nothing but thankful for the "yes."

Dear Mr. Smith,

I received your note about the Christmas turkeys. Yes, I realize you haven't bought a plant from us for many years. However, you gave me a job when I needed it the most. It is because of you and your willingness to take a risk that my company was able to survive all those years ago. It is because of you that I can keep hundreds of people employed today and work at a job I love. I owe you a huge debt of gratitude, Mr. Smith, and I will always send you a Christmas turkey.

Sincerely, Tom

Every year, customers could also count on a calendar of western art. At the bottom was the company name and address. The art resembled the artwork proudly displayed at the office and at home. T.H. Russell Co. was one of the first companies to send such a gift, and what a perfect item to show the personality of the owner. Not only was he an impeccable record keeper, but also a real cowboy.

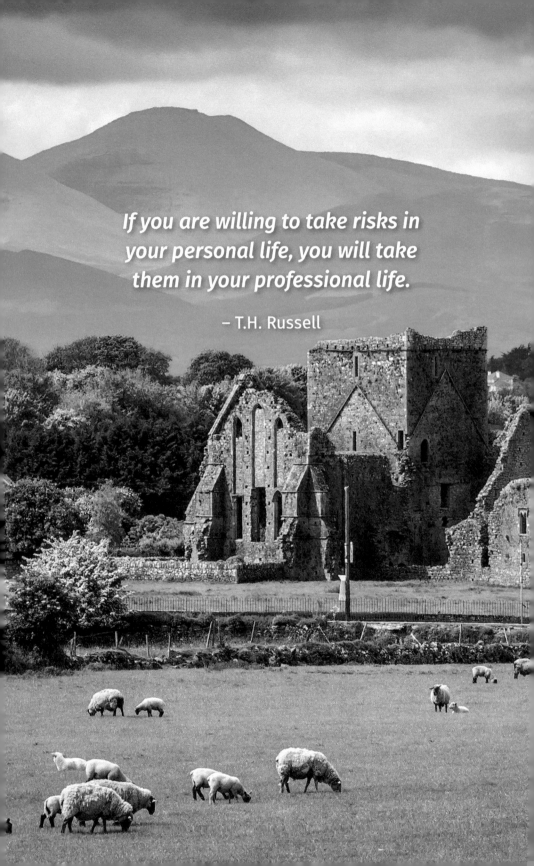

If you are willing to take risks in your personal life, you will take them in your professional life.

– T.H. Russell

Chapter 6
FAMILY

Home Front

Besides fashion and themed parties, Ginger was a pro at getting the best deal on groceries. Absolutely nothing was bought without a coupon. There was a lot of canned food, beans, potatoes, and mystery meat in their pantry, but a hot meal was always on the table at six o'clock, complete with dessert, because T.H. liked sweets. There was no junk food in the pantry, and we weren't wearing any new clothes to school, but it was understood among the children to don your best hand-me-downs and make that bus in the morning, because you weren't staying there!

Despite being buried behind piles of dishes and loads of laundry, Ginger somehow made it work and always looked stylish doing it. If you were hungry enough to want a snack, with apples at 59 cents for four pounds. you could guess what it was. "There are lots of fuzzy little squirrels looking in the window that would love to have that apple. It will make you able to run as fast as the wind," she would coo while tickling the hungry child.

Ginger was always resourceful. Any leftover apples went into a sweet cobbler and bananas into bread. Born during the Depression herself, she made sure nothing was wasted. "Darling, when I was a little girl, when it snowed, it snowed on my bed. Do you want to know what I did? I would make snow ice cream with a little extra cream and sugar *borrowed* from the corner diner," she would tell her children. Her purse was always full of those little sugar packets from restaurants. Our only medicine was white peppermints. Those little white candies were the "cure-all" for everything... plus fresh air, sunshine, and positive thinking!

Maternal Era

Uncle Joe moved in with Grandma Ann to care for her. He had a bathroom installed downstairs at 16th and Trenton so she could have easier access. The large family enjoyed getting together for Sunday Mass. All six of T.H. and Ginger's kids had been baptized as babies, three in Texas and three in Oklahoma. "I remember Mom always pinning a napkin to my head for Mass because I didn't have a veil," Jenny recalls.

"Oh, my mother and sisters wouldn't set foot inside the church without a head covering," Tom would agree.

Ann passed from a stroke in 1978.

During Ann's life, Stephanie remembers, "As soon as she opened the door, the delicious aroma of blueberry muffins surrounded you." Inside the home was the light, floral scent of her Laughter perfume. Here and there were family photos and a picture of President Kennedy. "Dad, are we Republican or Democrat?" a young Steffy asked. "I vote for the one that I think is going to do the best job," T.H. answered. "Is Grandma a Democrat?" she followed up. "Haha," he chuckled. "She is Catholic."

* * *

The cousins always came through whenever there was any situation—illness, a family event, or even working cattle at the ranch. As sacramental marriages became more and more uncommon, ushers at weddings would joke, "Are we supposed to be seating anyone on the other side?"

Aunt Pat kept an updated list of all the family's information. She held a Christmas party around the holidays, always featuring punch "with a kick" and punch "without." A few times the coffee table was moved over to make a country-western dance floor. The Bradleys held a St. Patrick's Day party for a time with lots of food, including green shamrock cookies for fun. The Funks put together a reunion at McNellie's downtown to catch up. It's always fun when our families get together. Crock-Pot corned beef and cabbage has always been a family favorite. Maureen showed up with her homemade potato soup one time, and it was a lifesaver, since the corned beef dried up while we were at the monastery, and we had almost burnt the cabin down.

During events at the house, the little kids would run all over the place, but not by the table, where the adults would sit and talk. Ann kept a chest upstairs with just a couple of toys inside. It was a race upstairs to get your hands on one, as they went quick! Outside in our tattered Sunday-best dress clothes, the kids would roll down the hill surrounding the house, which seemed like a mountain!

It was kids, kids, kids, laughter, and lots of time outside. We didn't need much yard. We didn't need anything. We made our own fun, and we respected the hierarchy. You didn't mess with the older kids. No matter how fast you could run, they could outfox you, and you would be sorry. And you never disturbed the adults.

* * *

The Funk family arranged a reunion tour of the 16th and Trenton house in 2013 with the gracious current owners. We all, adults and grandkids, rolled down the hill for ole time's sake. It seemed like a tiny hill to us now in the modest-sized yard. Tom took us into the basement to show where his beer processing plant had been. The upstairs window remains slightly opened, just the way Grandma always liked it. The wooden floors creaked when we walked across them. Afterward we all walked up to Andolini's Pizzeria for lunch and more reminiscing about what a happy and HUGE family grew up there.

"Dad, are you full-blood Irish?" Steffy asked.

"Ha, I'm full of drive to get the job done. Let's go eat" he answered.

"You are full-blood!" she exclaimed.

"You didn't mention it back when Irish were put at the bottom of the hay bale chute, because that guy often got killed standing there. We were expendable," he told her, recalling the stories.

* * *

T.H. and several of his siblings traveled to Ireland once during the 1990s to visit the Emerald Island. They searched all around for gravesites. Not being able to find any familiar names, they asked a guide. He said, "Aye, follow meh." They walked for several blocks off the beaten path, past nicely decorated Protestant graveyards adorned with ornate iron. "Har ye arr." He pointed around an isolated corner. "When we saw the poor little section surrounded with hand-placed stacked rocks just ankle-high and graves marked with popsicle sticks tied together, we knew we were in the right spot." There they buried Aunt Pat's house keys, which she had always carried with her.

* * *

After the matriarch Grandma Ann passed, so did the large Irish-Catholic family traditions. Holidays became about Santa Claus and the Easter Bunny, but they brought candy, cool presents, and money hidden in plastic eggs, so we let 'em hang. The shelves were stocked with Encyclopedia Britannica. We received the monthly *National Geographic* and *Reader's Digest*, as well as the Sunday *Tulsa World*, which provided Ginger with her coupon supply. Nothing made it to the table that wasn't bought at a discount. Dinners brought an awareness and appreciation to sit down together and discuss interesting topics. Never ever in front the of the TV!

THERALEE

"I don't do houses with kids or pets," the housekeeper interviewee explained.

"I don't blame you!" Ginger confirmed just as a dog went tearing through the room, chasing a cat.

"Mom! Tell them to leave me alone," a kid yelled from the other room. SLAM! went a door.

"I prefer nonsmoking homes," Theralee stated.

"Me too," Ginger agreed.

The cat came slinking back into the room, having defeated the slobbering, obnoxious dog, and hopped right into Theralee's lap. She threw her hands up in the air with an *argh* as the cat made a circle, then curled up in her lap for a nice nap. "I don't think this is the right job for me," she said.

"What would you like for me to have on hand for you to eat at lunch?" Ginger asked with a pen ready to make note of her preference.

"Are there any other pets?" Theralee inquired, looking around.

"Oh, uh, just a little harmless fish…and a bird that stays in its cage…most of the time." Ginger eased out the information.

"Hmm. This is a long drive for me," Theralee wavered.

"Then how about just once a week?" Ginger offered.

Theralee shooed the napping cat off her lap, stood up, and brushed off her skirt. She looked at the housewife with her purse in one hand and the other on her hip, as if to say, "Give me one good reason why I should work here."

With a deep sigh, Ginger pleaded, "Okay, it's a zoo. There are a bunch of animals here too!"

Theralee started to walk toward the door. "I'm going to have to think about this," she said doubtfully.

"Grand! The opening is immediate. I will see you next week!" Ginger sprang to her feet and extended her grateful "we have a deal, right?" hand.

Theralee shook hands, opened the door to leave, then turned to Ginger and said, "Is that child supposed to be tied to a tree?"

It wasn't unusual to come home and find Theralee up on a chair, wielding her broom and shrieking, "Ick! Get! Get! Ugh!" with one or two of the family ferrets underneath, leaping in the air and swinging off the end of the broom like it was a fun game. Theralee also often had to use her broom to break up fights between the kids. She would hold it like a barrier in between the quarrelers. "Whoever throws the next hit is going to hit the broom!" she would threaten.

She was never late, never called in sick, and stayed with Ginger for over two decades. Talk about a "good hand"! The house would stay sparkly (and peaceful) for about a whole happy hour after she left. She was a lifesaver to Mom and grandmotherly caring to the kids. Her presence in the home was serene, as she would quietly hum to herself while she worked. Ginger would have to hide her preferred lunch—a can of Coke and ham lunchmeat—from the kids. We would look all over the place for that Coke. We never did find her hiding spot!

You could set your watch by Theralee's quick break to eat and watch part of her "story" on TV. No matter what insanity was going on around her, and there was usually a lot, she maintained her professionalism. Although, I'm sure if it weren't for her endearing loyalty, she would have rather worked anyplace else. When she became too ill to work, T.H. left a check in the usual spot every Wednesday for her daughter to pick up so she could continue to go to school. Theralee's presence was definitely missed in our home.

Broken Bones and Broken Home

"Why are you lying on the couch, Matt?" T.H. asked one day.

"I crashed my motorcycle, and I think I broke my leg," Matt answered, wincing from pain in his supine position.

"I think you better be fine by tomorrow and break a sweat," T.H. warned.

Three days later, T.H. went out to the garage to look at the motorcycle. The gas tank was completely dented in.

"Let's go, son," T.H. instructed.

"Where?" Matt asked.

"To the doctor. I think you broke your leg, and you're going to need a cast and some crutches, because you're behind on your chores."

Even with one leg, Matt found a way to do his chores and mow lawns for extra cash. He would lay on the couch with his money fanned out on his chest and nap…with one eye open. When the younger three siblings tried to sneak in and snatch a bill, he would rouse and start swinging his crutch around, trying to whack the pesky little thieves. He liked the added challenge of his predicament. If one did manage to get some money, they wouldn't make it too far. Not only could Matt do his chores with one leg, he could hop faster than a kangaroo!

* * *

What seemed like a routine day at the big house changed with a phone call. It was St. Francis Hospital. T.H. had just crashed his Harley. It was a common joke around the house when T.H. left on his bike on occasion that Ginger would say, "I think it's going to rain today." "Well, then, I won't have to wash it!" he would grin and vroom off. On this particular day, as he was driving home in the rain, a car didn't see him and pulled out in front of him.

"Okay, get in the car, kids," Ginger mumbled as she hung up the phone. The kids sensed this wasn't a usual errand. The mood was somber. Some neighbors were driving by as we were quietly (for once) climbing into the family station wagon.

"Sorry about your dad," a little girl hollered out the window.

"Huh?" one of us said.

"We drove by and saw him lying in the street. His bike looks like a crumpled piece of paper. There is glass and metal everywhere. He was covered with a towel, but we knew it was him because we saw his cowboy boots sticking out. He wasn't moving. I think he's dead."

He had been knocked unconscious, had a broken hand, had sucked his tobacco into his lungs, and was pretty banged up. A large crowd was gathered around his hospital bed, hoping for him to wake up. The only sound was the *beep-beep-beep* of the machines.

The silence was broken with a sudden, "Hi, Jimbo!" from T.H.

"Boy, you look ugly as hell," Big Jim said with a laugh of relief. They immediately started cracking jokes and talking shop. "Don't you have the sense not to ride around in the rain? We have work to do!" Big Jim teased.

If you are ever hurting for a fun time, take as many kids as you can fit into a station wagon grocery shopping for the experience of a lifetime. Ginger pulled up into the drive after one such trip while T.H. was still recovering in the hospital. She could see a man sitting on the swing in the front yard. "Who is that?" she wondered out loud. It looked like Uncle Joe. Maybe he was in town to visit his brother in the hospital.

As they got closer, Ginger and the kids realized it was T.H.! "What are you doing here? You should be in the hospital," Ginger exclaimed.

"Well, I checked myself out. Open the door, please. I have work to do," T.H. said with gauze and tape stuck all over him.

* * *

The company was well underway, and Ginger was ready to retire. All she had ever wanted was to be a wife and a mom…and do it in style. She maintained that she "wouldn't have picked any other father for my six kids," and she will always be "Wonder Woman" to them. I guess reality is, she was only human, like the rest of us. Despite all the teamwork, we weren't exempt from broken bones and a broken home. Gone was the youngest-only protection, gone was the movie star off the set, gone was twenty-seven years with Tom. Gone was Mom.

CHORES, CHORES GALORE

Tom would come home from work and ask, "What's for dinner?" We would all stand around and look at each other. We ate a lot of Arby's, Hamburger Helper, and vanilla ice cream. He called it his "Mr. Mom days." His funny joke to keep spirits up was to act like the phone had rung, answer, and then be talking to the grocery store. "What? There's an emergency in the freezer department? I better come down right away and check on this situation!" Sometimes one of us would get to ride on the back of his blue Harley for one of these code-red runs! It wouldn't have mattered if we had been going to pick up a can of expired green beans. We were with DAD!

The dreaded dry erase board on which chores were written doubled to include not only everything outside but inside too. One time Glenn wanted to go hang out with his friends, and T.H.'s answer was "Sure, after you do the whole yard."

Glenn started the trimmer and let it buzz until the battery died. "I got a good start, Dad. The trimmer ran out on me. I'm charging it back up, and I'll finish it later," he reported.

T.H., without looking up from his study, said, "That's okay, son. Here, you can finish the job with these." And he handed Glenn a pair of scissors from his desk drawer.

When T.H. got home from work and you heard his cowboy boots hit the entryway, you knew you had exactly eleven steps to get out of town, and you knew which route to take. He was going to go straight to the thermostat, and it better not have been moved one degree. Next was the dry erase board to make sure all chores had been crossed off. It must be admitted here that *sometimes,* with Russell boys around, the girls were spared a bit. At the end of the long, long chore list, the board said "Girls—be pretty."

CUT THE MUSTARD

This phrase originally came from a man named O'Henry in 1891 who wrote short stories in the Galveston newspaper. It became a common saying around the big house. It didn't matter if you were a kid, a relative, an employee, or all of the above—you had better "cut the mustard."

Jenny was doing some expediting work for T.H. At the young age of sixteen or so, she would be sent to shops all over town to deliver drawings and check on progress. "Go sit in their office until they give you what you came for," T.H. would instruct her. He didn't mess around when it came to getting what was owed so his team could do what they needed to do to get paid. Even with the likes of Mr. Wayne Rumley at R&R Engineering. He is now a Tulsa University 2014 Hall of Famer himself, with top designs for a fabrication firm for air-cooled exchangers.

"He is turning off the lights," Jenny whispered to T.H. from a phone in the lobby by Rumley's office.

"So?" he replied.

"Well, what do I do?"

"I already told you what to do," he answered just before she heard a click and a dial tone.

It took some navigating to get past guards to be as close as possible to those corner offices, a lot of long days, and a little nodding off. But it was understood—sit there until he gives you what you came for.

The next phone call to T.H. came from Mr. Rumley himself. Wayne was behind finishing an air cooler. "What does it take to make your daughter leave here tonight so I can go home?" he asked T.H.

"Finish the job" was the matter-of-fact answer.

* * *

T.H. would visit jobsites in the field, walk around, talk to everyone, and observe. It would take a while for word to get around that he was the "boss man." By the time the superintendent found out T.H. was there, he would have already made his assessments. Not only did he enjoy hanging

BEER ON THE BUS

out in the field and meeting people, he was always looking for good hands. People were often astonished that the man who had just hung out, cracked jokes, picked up a wrench, and crawled down a dark hole with them was the owner.

"I enjoy this kind of work, and I like getting my hands dirty," T.H. would comment. "Sometimes people think they have to act differently when they find out who you are. I am no different." In his dusty cowboy boots and jeans, you wouldn't know he had a dime to his name, until he asked, "Do you want to come and work for me?" The flattered prospect would drop their tools and go climb into his blue pickup truck.

He was getting the best in the industry, and T.H. Russell Co. was getting the reputation behind the name. Even later, when his three mechanical engineer sons would came aboard, they started in the drafting department, learning about the business. "Call him T.H., not Dad" was the advice passed down from one to the other. It was business, professional with mutual respect, although they were a "work family" and had lots of fun. You proved yourself and earned your way in and up. No "shoo-ins."

* * *

The younger kids would sometimes accompany T.H. to work. The draftsmen would let us climb up on their laps to draw on their big white papers. They would flip over an important drawing to reveal a blank sheet and hand us a pencil. "We would go back to Dad's office, climb up in the big leather chair, and look around. Wow, this is where all the important decisions are made," Mandy remembers. There would be a glass with a little whiskey and some melting ice in it, as well as a smoldering cigar in a tray.

In the desk drawer, the kids could always find a pack of Black Jack (licorice-flavored) chewing gum. The shop had huge cranes with remote controls hanging down on a cord; we would take turns swinging as high as we could on those. We always found ways to pass the long hours of the day and entertain ourselves. On one trip to Louisiana, Glenn and Matt drove the field crew crazy. The superintendent politely suggested that "I bet the boys would have more fun at the hotel." T.H. came back to the hotel room later to find a note the boys had left: *Room service, please bring the shrimp out to the pool.*

* * *

T.H. would also visit his professors at his alma mater, TU, and ask for their star pupils. They would give him some "kid" in a baseball cap. T.H. would hire him and train him. He would be able to take about ten years' worth of knowledge and cram it into about two years of experience. The "kid" would soon be doing the work of a "senior" processing engineer. He believed the older employees had a duty to train the younger ones. He was talented at developing technical expertise and management style in people. But if you ask him, he denies it and gives all the credit to others. He instantly knew how to bring out the best in people, help them develop their God-given talents and find their strengths.

Outsiders Inside the Big House

Was a piece of bacon off someone else's plate really worth getting your hand stabbed with a fork? Depends—how badly did you want it? I still can't imagine where people get the idea that the Irish are so unruly? Without a mom around and with Dad always at work, it was pretty much a zoo without any safe zones. We did learn not to steal! It was Fight Club every day that ended in Y. Some valuable survival tricks:

1. Test what flinches—that will be what they strike with. Circle like a shark. After a strike, keep advancing pressure until subdued. Never jump back, surprised, as if to say "your turn."
2. If there is more than one sibling trying to get you, keep your back against something. Don't let them get behind you. Never lose eye contact with your opponent.
3. When being chased, master the art of throwing chairs (or anything) down behind you as you run. Remember, when chasing, if they glance a certain direction, they are going to go that way.
4. If you could make it behind a door to lock, that gave you just enough time to catch your breath. It wouldn't be long until the predator got fed up with trying to break the door down and decided to go around to devour the trapped prey. Quickly, straight out the window. Otherwise you're trapped for a long time.
5. Golden Rule = Crazy wins every time! It doesn't matter who is bigger or stronger...just crazier.

Russell family in Ireland

"*Don't worry, my daughter will jump, I just know it.*

– Tom Russell

Chapter 7

FUN

Skydiving

Speaking of crazy, T.H. once took Jenny, Matt, and Glenn on an "adventure" without telling her what it was. They knew she would *not* want to do it, and they were right.

Matt and T.H. climbed out on the wing of the airplane and disappeared into thin air. Glenn was edging his way out of the airplane onto the wing, trying to make it look painless for Jenny. He turned to her and smiled, but the wind shear totally distorted his face! He hung from the wing strut with feet dangling. In his selfless way, Glenn was showing her, "See just do this, and you will be fine." He let go, and POOF, he was gone!

Jenny was left alone in the plane with the pilot, who made a few circles at 4,000 feet in the air. "Ma'am, we're

getting low on fuel. You have to jump, or we have to land."
She dreaded a walk of defeat off that plane if she chickened
out more than she feared falling to her death. T.H. was on
the ground, proudly proclaiming, "Don't worry, my daughter
will jump, I just know it." Jenny was up in the air, mustering
the courage, thinking, "I'm going to fall to my death, I just
know it." She made peace with it, closed her eyes, and let go.
Anything was better than disappointing T.H. "You need to
work on your dismount," Tom instructed Jenny.

She didn't open them until the parachute opened
above her. Her anticipation of slamming into the ground
was pleasantly replaced with a sudden floating sensation.
The relief was fleeting, as she figured this was just going
to prolong the inevitable. Although she had been taught
how to steer, her mind was a blank as she soared and tried
to get some oxygen back into her lungs. The ground crew
jumped in the van to chase after her. She crash-landed on
the runway, flipping end over end until she finally felt her
momentum stop and her chute floated down all around her.
She couldn't see anything, but all of a sudden felt her body
being dragged hurriedly across the ground. The plane was
landing, and she was right in the path!

T.H. and the boys were waiting at the base when the van pulled up to deliver her. The doors flew open, and Jenny came tumbling out. Her body was still in shock. She had mud and grass crammed in the face shield of her helmet and could hardly speak or walk. The boys ran up clapping, cheering, and patting her on the back like she was Maverick from *Top Gun*. It took about half the drive back before she could form words and get them out of her mouth. "You guys sure know how to show a girl a good time!" she scoffed.

Oklahoma Lakes

Oklahoma is known for its lakes! It has the largest number of lakes created by dams in the U.S. Out of over two hundred, only two are natural. All the rest are man-made.

T.H. bought a sailboat—blue, of course—and taught himself how to sail. He nicknamed it his "Little Dinghy." He was sure not to get anything with a propeller! He was also sure to get one wet bike with lower horsepower than the other to cut out the "racing," or so he thought. He should have known that the boys would find a way for one to fall off and promptly get run over by the other while racing.

"Do we need life jackets, Dad?" Mandy asked. He was backing his boat down the ramp.

"What for?" he asked with a cigar dangling from his mouth, wearing his T.H. Russell Co. logo ballcap and Ray-Ban glasses.

"For the lake," Mandy clarified.

"Sure!" he exclaimed. "Then you can go and get the birds some wings too." He went back to unloading his boat, and all the kids piled out and jumped in the lake. Being raised by a man, we didn't have lunches packed, snacks, or sunburn prevention. Or anyone saying, "Be careful!" or "Bring a dry change of clothes." We just went. We even rode in the back of the truck down the highway to get there.

Much like the idea that one could fly by jumping off a ledge with an umbrella, the older kids convinced the younger ones that if they put on flippers and stood on the edge of the dock, holding on to a rope, then they would be skiing behind a wet bike in no time. Well, that doesn't work either. We sled behind the car around the hilly, snowy neighborhood. Anything that could go could also pull more passengers behind it.

Play wouldn't end until we ran out of gas and the sun went down. We would come dragging in late at night, soaked, dirty, burnt, and always HUNGRY!

TU Chemical Engineering Advisory Board

In 1981 (less than two years after its founding) Shannon Melton asked T.H. to join the TU Chemical Engineering Board. He was also a member of the Circle Society and the President's Council at TU. He joined other successful alumni to meet twice a year with students about the program. The group helped fund the school's first computer lab in '91, equipment for the unit operations lab, and endowment scholarships. In addition to financial support, the board contributes to the curriculum and course objectives.

"What I took into that room was all the good hands that I worked with. I could only do what I did because they were so good at what they did," T.H. remarked. "When anyone asks me what the secret to my success is,

I have to admit, 'The people I worked with.'" He got all his education at TU, all his experience on the job, and all his success from finding the best hands in the business. His answer to another question is equally flattering. When asked how to be a good parent, he answers, "Easy, you just have good kids."

In 1993 T.H. was inducted into the Science Hall of Fame. He was honored for his outstanding accomplishments in energy innovations and contributions to TU. The school stated that he "leads to an enriched future for the nation and the world" and "inspires others to pursue rewarding and challenging careers in all engineering and natural science fields." Riding along in the car on the way to the ceremony, Steffy asked, "Dad, are you famous?"

"I'm just a little fish in a big pond," he responded.

ROCKPORT AND MULE BARN

"Down in the west Texas town of El Paso, I fell in love with a Mexican girl...and Fellina would whirl," Marty Robbins belted from the Winnebago full of people and homemade party mix rumbling down the road. Friends from Marquette, Captain Bill and Joan Rowe, lived in Rockport, enjoying their time sailing. Big Jim and T.H. went in on a summer vacation home near theirs.

T.H. and Captain Bill

Bill was having trouble turning on the right street to find his house, so he painted a vertical white stripe on the curb to mark his turn. T.H., being the prankster he is, painted a matching stripe on his curb. Bill thought he had accidentally marked the wrong curb, so he put two vertical stripes on the right curb to mark his turn. This went on up to five stripes, until T.H. got busted paintbrush in hand.

* * *

During a sailing trip, T.H. decided he was "burning too much daylight" on the boat and wanted off to go back home and work. He dragged his suitcase from below and sat with it on the deck. Bill asked him for a quick favor. While T.H. was performing his boat duty, Bill hooked his suitcase to a rope and hoisted it high up on the mast. When T.H. returned to his post, his suitcase was gone!

Traveling through security in the airport on the way home, (this was before 9/11, mind you) Bill was next in line to pass through the metal detectors. BEEP! BEEP! BEEP! sounded the alarms, and lights were flashing. T.H. had locked a padlock on Bill's belt loop. A year later, delivered in the mail to the big house, was a nicely wrapped gift box. Inside were Bill's shorts, which he had decorated. They had been burnt, the hems were cut and frayed, and the padlock was still attached to the belt loop.

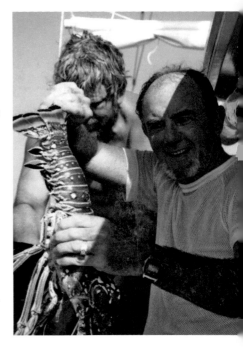

Big Jim, T.H. and a big lobster dinner.

* * *

Now, all kidding aside, these guys really looked out for each other.

For instance, once when Big Jim and Dolly were having a disagreement, T.H. went to their house to

150

smooth things over between them. "Well, tell him I said
___," Dolly would request of T.H. Jim would respond with,
"Tell her I said ___."

T.H. did what he could and then went to leave. As
he was pulling away, Jim had turned and was making his
way back up his drive with Dolly following a ways behind.
"Look out, Jim!" T.H. yelled to his buddy out the window.
Jim, just sure his wife was coming after him, (not knowing
what messages T.H. had really been delivering), dropped
to the ground and rolled under his boat in the driveway.
Jim lay on his stomach, frantically looking around for his
perceived attacker, while T.H.'s car drove off with roaring
laughter coming from it. His motto was, "We can find
things to fight about or, better yet, we can find things to
laugh about."

*　*　*

What is the best thing to do when driving eighteen
hours in the snow to go skiing, and there are flashing
signs that read, "*Monarch Pass is impassible. Turn back
now*"? The road is at 11,312 feet elevation, with mountain
on one side and sheer cliff on the other with no guardrail.

The pass marks a continental divide between the Atlantic and the Pacific Oceans. Well, if you ask T.H. and the boys, what you do is briefly stop in the middle of the dark, freezing night, put chains on the tires, and keep on trucking, of course!

"Dad, what's a millionaire?" Steffy asked, riding along.

"It means someone's net worth is equal to a million dollars," T.H. answered.

"Are you a millionaire?" she questioned.

"Ha! I just do what I think is right, and sometimes that pays off. It doesn't matter what we have. It matters what we do for other people," he responded without taking his eyes off the road.

She went back to reading her book, and he went back to building a gas plant in his head. Then she quickly glanced up at the other kids with a gleam in her eyes and smiled. The image was worth a million words.

* * *

The historic red Mule Barn in Crested Butte, Colorado, literally used to be a barn for mules. It was moved to the base of the ski resort of this old mining town and purchased by T.H. and Jim for winter vacations. It was within walking distance to the bus stop just down the street and also to the quaint downtown area of dining and shopping. The corner store sold Jelly Bellies out of a quarter machine.

How many people did the Mule Barn hold? As many as could fit in the beds, on the couches, and on the floor space. Glenn would sometimes bundle up and sleep outside to keep the kids off him, but they would eventually find him, getting past all his booby traps. That's how he got the handle "booby chief."

T.H. hitting the slopes in Crested Butte.

"First chair up and last chair down" after "calisthenics" at the crack of dawn were the marching orders. Riding up on the gondola all the way to the summit, T.H. would look out at the scenic, snowy view and recite his favorite poem, "The Cremation of Sam McGee."

"And there sat Sam...in the heart of the furnace roar;
And he wore a smile you could see a mile, and he said:
   "Please close that door....
Since I left Plumtree, down in Tennessee, it's the first
   time I've been warm."

Everyone had a "ski handle" (which was pretty much a roast session) and we were divided up into cooking teams. Each team got one night to cook and clean, and the trip ended with a culinary vote on the best meal. With as many mismatched hand-me-down layers as you could fit under a black-and-white T.H. Russell Co. logo jacket, rental skis, and a smashed PB&J in your pocket, it was off to Paradise Bowl. "Smokin' Joe" always had a reliable trail map and the best route planned, but you better hurry up if you wanted to know what it was. We didn't call him "Smokin'" for nothing! Neal carved his own trail through the trees, earning him the handle of "Bushwhacker."

Captain Bill Rowe, Bob Funk & T.H.
The Mule Barn '83 Cook-Off winners.

When the Ruby Chief run was sheer ice, which it often was, we had to slide down on our rear ends…

straight into the warming hut. There was a big jump in the bowl that was the site of an ongoing jumping contest. "Mass momentum," Jim would say as he whizzed by in his tuck. Speaking of contests, it was here that "Twister Tom" just happened to catch Bill,

T.H. on a hiking and camping trip.

the "Silver Queen," and his family's hilarious wipeout on his video camera. It was so funny it ended up winning $10,000 on *America's Funniest Home Videos*. When T.H. was snapping his boots into his skis, he would rattle them, and say "Whoa, easy now. Watch out, once these babies see the mountain, they take off!"

Not so funny was when Mandy lay in the clinic with a broken arm, and part of the group busted in to lend comfort…by videotaping the snot frozen to her face and heckling her. The doors flew open, sending a burst of freezing air into the clinic and the hecklers. Clomping in on snow-covered boots with a frozen beard, Matt the "Ice Man" said, "Good job. I guess you won't be needing this," and lifted her ski pass from around her neck. "Any way you could stuff some extra gauze in her mouth, Doc? She can be a real whiner," Glenn remarked.

Glenn reached up for the pass and was put in a headlock. *Zip* went Mandy's jacket pocket.

"What are you doing?" she demanded.

"Looking for your Snickers bar. You won't be needing that either," Glenn scoffed. *Zip.* "Where is it? Or did you already feed it to your little princess face?"

They all went wrestling out the door, fighting over the goods, laughing, pushing, and shoving. "How did you even get going fast enough to break something, anyway?" they hollered over their shoulders.

"You have an interesting family," the doctor commented.

BACKPACKING AND SCUBA DIVING

Uncle Joe, who was living on the East Coast in Washington, D.C., met us to hike part of the

Appalachian Trail and, later the Needleton Mountains in Colorado. *Choo–choo*, the train from Needleton chugged off into the woods and eventually disappeared. It wouldn't be back for a week.

While everybody prepared, the boys went down the line, lifting all the hikers' packs to test the weight. If a pack tested too heavy, they reached in and tossed unnecessary items to the ground. They looked like taller, bearded Yodas from the Star Wars movie, going through Luke Skywalker's stuff. "You don't need this," they would say as something was flung overhead.

Once the pack met specifications, it was hoisted onto the hiker's back, and Neal would thrust a rain poncho over the top. With a quick spin around and

T.H., Matt & Glenn scuba diving in Cozumel, Mexico

swift slap on the back, the hiker was pointed in the direction of the trail, which looked like it went straight up into the oblivion.

"Where do I go?" the first in line asked.

"Up to the all-inclusive resort for your massage," Matt answered.

"There is a resort up there?" the lead anxiously asked.

"No! But there are six-foot timber rattlesnakes, so watch where you step," Glenn warned.

We had to hang our food in trees each night to keep the black bears off of it and hope they weren't hungry enough to eat us. Nothing makes you appreciate the comforts of home like camping.

* * *

Rolling up the Mexican coast in a cab, T.H. had a map on his lap, a pen in his hand, and was doing calculations. "A dónde, Señor Thomas?" the driver asked.

As the town got farther and farther away, one of the kids asked, "Dad, should we have a dive master?"

"What for?" he responded.

"So we know what to do," the young scuba diver replied.

"You swim around and look at the fish, that's what you do," T.H. explained, and into the ocean we jumped to float down the coast with the current! After a "three-hour tour," we emerged like sea creatures from the ocean, crusted with salt. We sheltered our sopping wet equipment in the bushes, then sat on the side of an isolated dirt road in what bit of shade we could find until a cab eventually came along.

* * *

During a dive at a beautiful coral reef, the divers were all passing around an octopus. Its soft body slowly

The fearless navigators—
T.H., Matt & Glenn

crawled from arm to arm, slightly swaying with the current and looking at you with dark intelligent eyes. When it was T.H.'s turn, he felt the sensation of the suction cups on its tentacles attaching to him. He gave a little jiggle to signal to the creature to go ahead and move on. "El Ocho" was quite happy hanging on to his arm. It was giving the intriguing bubbling man ample time to take in this incredible encounter.

T.H. shook his arm with a little more vigor to assure the creature that their meeting had been adjourned. Ocho wrapped his tentacles around his arm and held on even tighter. T.H. became annoyed with the close encounter and started flailing, violently thrashing his arm back and forth, causing quite a commotion. All of a sudden, the water went dark. When the ink dissipated and visibility returned, we were all looking around at each other, wondering what had just happened. Ocho had vanished. T.H.'s usually smiling, happy face was contorted and thoroughly perturbed.

The divers started spindling to the surface like dolphins in an air show to spit their regulators out of their mouths, take a huge gulp of air, and bust out laughing. Bobbing all around the surface were dark heads howling in a pod. One by one, we crawled onto the boat, gasping for air, reaching for each other's gear and helping people up the ladder. No one could even speak, only laugh!

A diver finally managed to form a sentence. "What went so wrong, Dad?"

"It was on me, and I didn't like it!"

Too bad we didn't get that one on video, or it would have been another *Funniest Home Videos* winner. As all fish (or mollusk, in this case) stories do, it eventually grew into, "It was trying to grab my dive knife and steal my watch. I had to fight it off like the Loch Ness monster, and you goofballs were no help!"

YMCA

From goofballs to handballs, T.H. was always active. He made sure all six kids got exposure to all types of sports. He would often enroll us in some sport and then have to kick us out onto the court or field at the Young Men's Christian Association for healthy "body, mind, and spirit." We all tried just about everything they had to offer…at least once.

T.H. played in handball tournaments at the Y during the '80s and has several trophies to show for it. It is a sport in which players use their hands to hit a small, hard rubber ball against a wall (inside an enclosed 40' by 20' half court) in such a way that the opponent hopefully cannot do the same without the ball touching the ground twice. Spectators could sit on the bleachers outside the court to watch through the Plexiglas, but only after you had practiced your racquetball or done "something constructive." It wasn't a fancy country club, but it was a "do something constructive to better yourself" club.

Russia

The *Tulsa World* reported on 9-20-1992 about T.H. Russell Co. building and sending a refinery to the cold, impoverished island of Sakhalin (just north of Japan) that was "desperately trying to revitalize its oil industry to generate hard currency." Hub Ferrell was the vice president of the company at the time. There were thirty employees in the office and fifty more at the shop. The new mini-refinery at Sakhalin produced 1,500 barrels of diesel and jet fuel that was sent via pipeline to the mainland. This plant not only produced product, it produced hundreds of jobs for Sakhalin island residents.

Jim's Mohawk Steel built a massive heater for the refinery. Delivery and installation was a challenge, since the island was subject to severe winters, blocking all travel except by air. Boats got as close as they could to the island before the ice got too thick. From there, they moved the equipment across on giant sleds. Military helicopters were used every morning to blow the snow off the skids. The situation was further complicated by years of bureaucracy and the end of the Cold War making the area very unstable.

Being the largest country in the world, Russia has eleven time zones and six languages: Russian, Chinese, Arabic, French, English, and Spanish. What seemed like a "Mission: Impossible" wasn't for a country that had sent the first man, Yuri Gagarin, into space, and it wasn't impossible for T.H. Russell Company either. Russia's main exports are energy (oil, petroleum, gas, and coal).

Some Russians came over to the States after the plant was complete to visit, and they brought some specialty vodka (chilled, of course). They held it up and said, "Neat." We took the bottle to look at the interesting label and said, "Yes, neat," handing it back. They then passed us a plastic cup of vodka. "Neat, yeh." We finally figured out that "neat" meant "straight." This was the traditional way to taste vodka, not over ice or mixed with anything.

"Rugby," one of them said, producing a ball and tossing it up from his palm. They taught us how to play, and even with the language barrier, we managed. Those capable, tough engineers managed just fine out at the Ranch and didn't even flinch when they dipped into (what us Okies think is freezing cold) Spring Creek. "Ah, yeh, is good!" they remarked as they swam around.

*Courage is being scared to death...
and saddling up anyway.*

– John Wayne

The Chapter 8
THE RANCH

THE RANCH

In the 1980s, T.H. Russell Co. purchased two areas of land (nicknamed Rocking C and Timberlake) in Cherokee County for cattle ranching and weekend retreats. And by "retreat," I mean rugged, rough country— lots of hard, physical labor—and *lots* of ticks!

T.H. AND HIS FAVORITE HORSE, POLE CAT "POLKY"

Snap crack clip-clop crunch! What was all that commotion coming from the woods next to the little cabin? All of a sudden, through the thick leaves and trees, a white Appaloosa horse with brown spots emerged, reins hanging down, the saddle vacant. It was T.H.'s horse, "Polky," but where was T.H.? Oh no, what had happened? Was he all right? How would we ever find him?

Searchers went running into the woods to look for him. The hills were steep, the rocks were sharp, and the brush was thick. Some fallen logs were so large they had to be climbed over after a quick glance checking for rattlesnakes on the other side.

T.H. and Polky

Snap crack crush crunch! Someone or something was coming toward us. The searchers froze to listen, making quick eye contact with each other to ask, "Do you hear that?" They frantically scanned the area for the best tree to shimmy up if it was a bear or bobcat looking for its next meal. A figure emerged from the dense brush. It was T.H.! He was alive! He also had blood streaming down his face and running down the front of his dirty shirt. That, my friends, was a typical day at the Russell Ranch.

Make My Day, Dirty Harry

Slap! Slap! "Look at that, I can set my whole finger in that gash!" said Uncle Willy. Glenn's .22 revolver quick draw was so quick that he shot himself in the leg before he got it out of his side holster. "Ah, that's nothing a little sip of whiskey and some salve won't fix."

"Argh!" Glenn winced as Willy poured Yukon Jack into the wound.

To be faster than the other guy in producing a plant and in gun battles paid off. Usually.

Rocket Riding & Explosions

No sooner had his leg healed up than Glenn went through the back windshield of a truck. Apparently, the driver doesn't steer too well when the guys in the bed are shooting bottle rockets at him inside the cab.

There might have been an occasional explosion or two. Just ask Neal. His whole body was set ablaze because someone didn't label the gasoline cans. I guess that's a no-no in the mechanical engineer's mind. The blast blew him back ten feet. After the flashbang, he came to and felt intense heat. He looked down with blurred vision to assess the blaze, and it turned out *he* was the blaze! Good thing he was good at quick thinking and good at the tuck and roll. Being the youngest of six, everything really did roll downhill.

Neal's severe wounds required seriously painful home scrubbing treatments. Sun visors came in handy for covering his face when he had to go into town. At stoplights it was difficult to ignore the obvious gawking of other occupants in nearby cars as they plastered themselves against the window, gasping and pointing, their screams of horror muffled by the glass.

"You aren't the same patient I saw last time!" the doctor exclaimed. "What have you done?" Ginger had suggested a home remedy of vitamin E and rose hip oil to treat his skin. It worked wonders! And, of course, to remind him about "positive thinking."

Bag Bash

Annually, the ranch is the site for Jenny's birthday "Beasties from Bishop Kelley Bash." When you attended BK, you didn't just graduate with preparedness for the next phase, you graduated with lifelong buds. This was a women-only gathering that has continued for decades to the present day.

Many wild tales and whisperings would circulate after said bash. One year, T.H. and the boys, who aren't easily impressed, decided to crash it to see what all the hype was about. They found the gals down at the creek, munching on Debbie's famous dill dip with pretzels, collecting pretty leaves and talking about the joys of being moms.

"Hey! What are you doing here?" they scoffed at the intruders. "No boys allowed!"

"Well, since you are here, will you build us a fire, please? We don't want to get all dirty collecting logs, and it's getting a little chilly," Renee requested. The event has been affectionately called "The Bag Bash" ever since. Of course, they were left with a magnificent roaring campfire beside a pile of perfectly sized, stacked logs to supply them all night long.

Neal building a bonfire for the "Bags."

RAM THE FORD

"They're tearing up the fence! Hurry! Do something!" Panicked shouts interrupted the mundane work during the heat of the day. Two rival bulls had grazed close enough in their respective pastures, and it was on before you could say, "How now, brown cow?"

T.H. drove his truck in between the raging bulls to separate them. They took a step back to size up this new, big, blue, metal "bull" that had just entered the ring.

170

With a lowering of their heads, snotty snorts, and hooves kicking up cupfuls of dirt—RAM! One of the bulls wasn't backing down and head-butted the driver's door.

The truck violently rocked from side to side. T.H. tilted his cowboy hat out the window to take a look at the huge crumpled indention in the side of the cab. With his smoldering cigar dangling out of his mouth, he said, "I should have just let them work it out instead."

Unhitched

It wasn't any surprise to see T.H. take on 2,000 lbs. or more with his truck. Once, after loading up with all the needed supplies to work the land, there was a huge CRASH! The trailer had come unhitched off the back of the truck and was standing vertically on its end, with the two front wheels spinning in the air and two flailing horses inside! Someone "who shall remain nameless" hadn't used the right size ball hitch to hook up the trailer.

With no hesitation, T.H. jumped inside the trailer with the thousands of pounds of freaked out horse. The trailer jerked from side to side and sounded like elephants trapped in a china cabinet.

Everyone stood gasping with their hands over their mouths, eyes wide, waiting to see if T.H. was going to come out alive, still processing the fact that *yes, he had just jumped right in there!*

The trailer rocked forward, and all 5,000 lbs. of livestock, metal, plus T.H. came crashing back down on all four wheels with a big bounce and loud metal BANG! T.H. emerged unscathed and looked in the back of the truck.

"Did you get the shovels?" he asked, looking around.

The spectators were still aghast. "What did you do?" someone piped up.

"What?" he said as he spun around. His expression showed that he wondered why he was hearing talk and not seeing walk. "Oh, I pulled on the one halter I could reach and eased 'em forward, and the other one followed. Let's go, we're burning daylight, and we have work to do."

It was several miles bumping down the dusty road before any of the "child labor crew" was able to take their first breath. No one was about to pipe up as to which one of us had hooked up the trailer with the wrong size hitch, didn't matter now. No more "burning daylight."

Moving a Mountain

Mandy stood in the heat, swatting flies, mosquitoes, and wasps the size of drones, and stared at a massive pile of rocks beside a fifty-foot-long and thirty-six-foot-wide wooden border. This was to be the site of a much-needed barn.

"This foundation will prevent sinking and wood rot," T.H. said.

"How are we going to move that mountain of rock? Is a front loader coming?" Mandy asked.

"Front loader? What would we need that for?" T.H. replied as he pointed to a rusty old wheelbarrow with clumps of dried cement stuck to it. "Here ya go," he said, handing her a shovel and a rake. "You take care of this. I have to go see about the cracked concrete slab. If that thing goes, we'll be crossing the creek by canoe."

That wasn't all that was cracking. Mandy's voice did a bit when she asked, "What do I do, Dad?"

"What do you mean? You make sure this is all level by the time I get back."

"Do you have any gloves?" Mandy stammered.

T.H. patted all around his torso and his pockets, front and back. "Hmm, where did I put those little matching princess gloves? I guess we left them on the float after your parade!" Tom kidded.

Vroom, the truck rumbled as he cranked it on. *"And it burns, burns, burns, the ring of fire,"* Johnny Cash crooned from the cab. As the truck bounced down the dirt road in a cloud of dust and out of sight, the music became fainter. *"The ring of fire…"* Leaving Mandy standing there alone to move a mountain by sundown.

* * *

The Ranch was where everyone came together, and nature came to you. It was also the site of many BBQs, parties, hayrides, and horseback rides. No matter rain, heat, or sleet, things got done. In typical T.H. fashion, no one said the forbidden word *can't.* They just knew there was an invisible sign on the gate that said, *"Come with a can-do attitude."*

It wasn't unusual to be riding horses deep in the country, lost, with leaves stuck in our hair, cockleburs stuck in our pants, and the sun going down. During one such ride, T.H. pulled out his topographic map. Jenny said, "Who are we kidding?" She pretended to blow her nose on it, threw it up in the air, and away they rode. When the going got tough, the tough had better "quit your sniffling and cowboy up," as Dad would say.

See, rules are a little different out in the country… as in, there aren't any, and there isn't any cell reception either. It was you, and it was the wild, and there was no place for "woofle cookies"! Some caves, ridges, and ravines were so deep, narrow, or steep that the only way out of them was to hop off, slap the horse on the rump, and crawl out on your hands and knees.

We never knew what was going to bust out to claim its territory and spook the horses. And horsey see, horsey do. When one blows, they all blow and go. You're better off up there than down there, playing the Hokey Pokey with pounding hooves. Unless you want a really long walk home, hang on…even if it's around the neck!

"Quit showing off your trick riding," T.H. would holler. "Should we charge admission for this amateur rodeo? Let's go, get control!"

MISS JETT

What is brown, beautiful…and fast? Miss Jett. What happens when you watch too many old western movies with your dad? You think it looks not only fun but also as easy as the Duke makes it look. Steffy decided to take Miss Jett for a spin. Let's put it this way: tornados have nothing on that mare. After Steffy got bucked off, Tweety Birds and stars were floating around in her vision. Rolling around on the ground, blubbering, she knew she had better get up.

The worst of it was there was no time to sit in the shade and recover. She had to get back on, lest T.H. find out! "Have courage and get back in that saddle. We don't lay around and feel sorry for ourselves!" she could imagine him saying. I wonder if that is why that horse was named Miss Jett, and why when Uncle Willy put on his boots to leave for chores, his parting words to the kids were, "…and stay off Miss Jett!"

Mr. Rooster

Of all the animals dealt with on the farm, such as bison, wild hogs with razor-sharp teeth, raccoons, snakes, longhorns, and even tarantulas, the meanest was definitely Mr. Rooster. You could be walking along, minding your own business, and hear a massive wing-flapping coming, creating a wind tunnel that would almost knock you off balance. It was a matter of seconds before you felt that sharp talon stab you every bit of 2-3 inches deep, then the familiar sensation of warm blood trickling down your leg. That bird that had just looked to be pecking around, appearing unconcerned when you passed, was waiting for his preoccupied victim to turn their back so he could launch his air attack!

Wild, Wild Horses

Coming across wild horses while on saddled horses was a real picnic in the park. It is on before you could say, "Whoa." With dirt flying, ear-piercing squealing, horses spinning like spheres, riders tried to hang on to a tornado that suddenly whiplashed back for front strikes and the

177

gnashing of teeth, then thrusting forward so the hind end could come up in attempts to land (45 mph, 2,000 pounds of pressure) power kicks on each other.

I've often said there's nothing better for the inside of a man than the outside of a horse.

– Ronald Reagan

"Unplug it! Unplug it!" was T.H.'s joke, referring to the electric horse rides outside the stores. "I was just hoping it would run out of quarters soon. That's about all you can do is ride it out…and win the fight," he would say.

Bobcats and Bags of Cement

It isn't eerie at all to have a 160 lb. predator slinking along a ridge, looking down at you and following for miles. "Here, kitty, kitty, kitty," Tom would mimic.

"Why isn't he sleeping right now? They're supposed

178

to be nocturnal," Jenny would question.

"He is looking at you and licking his chops, Dad," a rider would say, shifting the target.

"Do you think he can smell my granola bar?" Jenny asked.

"Well, he isn't getting my flask," Tom proclaimed.

Jenny, Rita and her shepherd.

"Wait a minute, you have a granola bar?" Mandy asked.

"Wait a minute, you have a flask?!" Jenny said.

HAY HOUSE

Hiking deep into the woods revealed a hidden oasis. The boys constructed a "Hay House." All the materials had to be carried in. Stacked square bales were bound by long wooden 2x2s twined to the large blocks of hay and secured at the top and bottom of the structure. Hay provides natural insulation and, covered with earthen plaster on both sides about 1-½" thick, provides protection from the elements. Space was left for a window and a door. Metal sticks to burlap better, so strips of it were placed behind where metal would make contact with the wood.

"I thought I was raising engineers, not the three little pigs!" T.H. joked. "While everyone else is out doing something constructive, I hope a wolf doesn't come along to huff and puff and blow your house down!"

Whenever T.H. thought that his kids weren't getting up early enough or getting enough done, he would say, "You know why family ranches are all convenience stores now? Because all the hands slept in."

Are We Going the Right Way?

Always the prankster, T.H. would spin around on his horse and come riding up beside the unsuspecting facing backward. "Are we going the right way? Are we there yet?" Then he would let out a Billy-the-Kid laugh and spin back around. I tell you one thing, horses always know the way home. It was proven many times in the pitch-dark when all we could do was hunker down, put a hand up to shield our face from come what may, and yell "HAH!" There aren't any Polaroids to prove it, but as far as Yeti goes…I believe!

Thistle Bushes

"I think God made thistle bushes so we would have a tiny taste of what hell would be like," Neal remarked. The robust bushes get two to five feet tall, with needle-sharp spines every bit of four inches long and a hook on the thicker end all over the stems. Sometimes in the middle of the night, the screams from the cabin stopped. A niece had one of those lovely spines go all the way through the rubber sole of her shoe and into her foot before it broke off. Talk about a "thorn in the paw." Neal didn't hesitate to retrieve his homemade medic kit to perform minor surgery in the dark cabin in the woods. See, out there you have to be the doctor, the logger, the vet, the law, the farmer, and the hunter, but with little kids, not the scout!

Scouting

Neal would send out eager, fearless scouts to the creek to find crossing. With the sun going down, the coyotes coming out to howl, and only the moon to light the way you know you aren't in the city anymore. Their figures got smaller and smaller, and the time between seeing them come out to go back in at a different spot was getting longer and longer, until they disappeared completely.

Mandy reached for the door handle but was stopped by the startling sound of a click.

"He is a young man, mama. Let him figure it out." Neal was strong and confident, not one bit rattled.

She leaned back in her seat, and they resumed talking about things, such as more than you would ever want to know about bear scat. Neal knew the hard way that boys had to face danger and respond with courage to become men.

"Brown with berries" meant just passing through. "Black without berries" was when you knew the bear had turned to meat and it was time for a Rosy roll call on the herd. "Starting August is when they're going to come in closer, looking for food as harvest starts to decline. Stay 'bear aware' until about November, when they find their cave for hibernation." Neal would explain the wilderness.

The scouts would return with a macho strut, a full report, and the most optimal place to cross.

KEEPING YOUR COOL

Flying high up in the air, was it a bird? Was it a plane? No, it was Mandy in a gas-powered parachute airplane! After circling a few times, she looked down and saw everyone running around frantically and waving their arms. It turned out the radio connection had gone out. Don't worry—all ground crew and pilots had been extensively trained and had thorough safety briefing. Okay, not so much. The way

The Russells on the Ranch

the Russells rolled (or flew) was just hop on and go, figure it out. Matt's last piece of advice before boarding was, "No matter what happens up there, sis, keep your cool, alright?"

"I looked down and saw Matt standing still, with his hands in his pockets, looking up at me," Mandy says. "He pursed his lips and slowly blew out as if he had a birthday candle." A calm came over her. She remembered what he had said, made another circle, went through a treetop, and landed. She knew that if this was it, it wasn't going to be by losing her cool in front of T.H. and the boys. Take that, Amelia Earhart!

SPRING CREEK

Spring Creek is a beautiful, crystal-clear, affectionately nick-named "fountain of youth." It is a thirty-four-mile natural spring that flows southwest right through both properties. "It will cure whatever ails ya," we always said. Spring Creek could be fifty degrees on a good day. Kind of like a spa...only a different brrr.

"Jump in. You will come out like a shiny new penny," any newcomer to the "polar bear club" would be told. Days at the creek included rope swings, watermelons, campfires, and searching for arrowheads left by the Clovis Indian tribe hundreds of years before. Records are hard to find. They had good reason not to trust the government, but their spirit is felt, their culture is admired, and their courageous warriors in battle are imagined. If you've never seen what a cottonmouth snakebite does to a person, you don't want to. Who knew a leg could come in that shade of purple? Or swell up that big? Even a dry bite from a rattler can hurt pretty good, but you didn't let one tear hit the floor to show it.

COUNTRY COTTAGE

What is it about the country? The stars are brighter, the air is fresher, and vegetation and wildlife are more abundant. A beautiful, fun-loving woman doesn't hurt either.

"She likes you, Dad," T.H.'s kids would remark.

"Nah, no way she does," he would reply and return to eating his burger and small bowl of ice cream. *"Tired, sweaty, clothes ripped, and covered in dirt…or no service,"* was how the "proper attire" sign on the door of the Country Cottage in town should have read. After a long, hard day's work, it was a common occurrence to crawl in there half-alive, filthy, and always HUNGRY!

If T.H. disappeared, you had to look around to find which corner the beautiful woman had him in, chatting. Pam, from the nearby town of Rose, had blond hair, a creamy complexion, and a contagious laugh. She was a waitress there and a single mom to two children, Ashley

A Note from Pam…

Tom introduced me to living life to its fullest.
Everyday with Tom is an adventure. Still to this day we can say our love for each other has no name 🤍.
Family is everything to both of us. We have worked and blended our families together which says a lot about each one of our children and bonus children we each have received. The personalities are endless.
Traveling was a great passion for Tom and I and all of our family. Our travels together include going around the world to visit World Heritage Sites from Manchu Pichu, Easter Island, Angkor Wat, Taj Mahal, Serengeti, Petra to Diving The Great Barrier Reef. Hiking in Canada and seeing my first Grizzly Bear up uncomfortably close. There was an adventure for everywhere we went. Among my favorite trips were with the Family. Our huge blended family, kids, and grandkids, usually not less than 32! Going to Ireland, Scotland, Train-trips, Beach Trips, Ski trips, Scuba diving and, Iceland! Traveling with Tom is a book in itself.
I am so blessed.
Pam, Mom, Bonus Mom, Pamma, Grandma, Grammy Gram, Grammy, and Grandma with all the glasses. These are all the names that have been bestowed on me.

Ann and Bobby Lee. She was a very capable country girl. T.H.'s blue eyes just twinkled when he looked at her, and vice versa. When a big bowl of ice cream appeared on the table, it was true love…he really liked her a lot too! T.H. started to have a spring in his step and a positively giddy attitude. Pam hopped on his Harley, they rode off into the sunset, and the rest is history. Okay, not exactly. She needed a little convincing that she wanted to matriarch this clan. Grab her don't let her get away!

Josh, Jessica, Pam, Neal, Clint & a grandson in Ireland.

Tom with bow and arrow.

You can't retire dad.
You support too many people.

– Tom's Kids

Chapter 9

THE THOMAS RUSSELL CO.

Hanlon Award

In 1997 T.H. won the most prestigious honor given in the petroleum industry. Midstream held the event in San Antonio, TX. All of T.H.'s and Pam's kids turned out to see him become the 61st recipient of the Hanlon Award. T.H. and his family got to meet Dick Cheney, who was the secretary of defense at the time and later became vice president of the U.S. from 2001–2009. Dr. Kenneth Hall, who has twelve inventor (or co-inventor) patents to his name, was there. As a researcher and professor, he has four patents involving the gas-to-liquids process alone. Mark Sutton was the staff adviser at the time. He has done tremendous work developing standards, conducting research, and educating the workforce. Not only did we have a great time on the Riverwalk, these leaders plus many guests were honoring Dad!

T.H. was awarded for perfecting techniques for building low-cost modular gas plants. His company had earned a reputation for integrity and efficiency. The president of GPA, Joe Becraft, told the large crowd gathered about T.H.'s reputation. "His plants are very hard to come by. Everyone wants them." He also explained how if T.H. and his company hadn't been doing their work, then "considerable amounts of natural gas and liquids might have been unprocessed, or worse, simply wasted."

T.H. had attended his first GPA convention in 1965. He'd never dreamed he would be standing on the stage someday. In 1965, the average wellhead gas price was 15 cents per thousand cubic feet. It was now at $2.00, and production was averaging seventeen trillion cubic feet per year. Gulf waters had been added that were once thought too deep for the drill bit. T.H. gave all the glory back to God, his TU professors, co-workers, customers, and family. The industry was thriving with new technology, expanding markets, and a steady supply of oil and gas.

RussKids, LLC

Time for an investment party like it's 1999! T.H. set up a family investment company at Bank of America with Mary Hale as our portfolio manager. We rotated holding leadership positions and had regular meetings. It was an educating time to explore the finer aspects of business, plan for retirement, and set the standard to share profits with charity. It was an opportunity to entrepreneur in areas other than gas processing, using the professional system and floor plan put in place by T.H.

We exposed ourselves to various situations, such as dividing into two teams and having an E-Trade contest. We hunkered and bunkered for Y2K. Although no new businesses spun off, Glenn led the way for us to invest in precious metals, platinum, silver, and gold. He wasn't happy with a certificate stating ownership of something unseen in some vault in New York, so he had Lloyd's of London insure the metals brought over in a guarded, armored truck for storage in the bank vault. It was such an exciting experience and a switch from dealing with "cyber cash" made possible by Glenn's extensive research and guidance.

191

Looking back over the notes and minutes of the meetings, one can see opportunities being presented, mentoring, and also a high expectation to "cut the mustard." It's easy to see a consistency behind the T.H. Russell name of doing the right thing and being charitable, either behind closed doors or behind open doors, whether one is related or not. The pulse of innovation and integrity is palpable when dealing with the likes of such an extraordinary man. He truly wills what is best for others and wants to help people succeed both personally and professionally.

THOMAS RUSSELL COMPANY 2003-2015

In the year 2000, Tom decided to retire and sell his beloved, twenty-nine-year-old T.H. Russell Company.

"You can't retire, Dad. You support too many people," his kids complained.

"Let's do it again, boss," his boys suggested.

"We need you in this industry," his contacts remarked.

After selling the company, Tom spent his three contractual "non-compete" years productively teaching at TU. He also taught for John Campbell Company, who sent him to Saudi Arabia for a challenging three months. "The oppression of the people, especially the women and the children, was disheartening. They are really smart. Those people have so much potential, and so does their country," he expressed. The religious persecution was all too familiar.

Saudi Arabia discovered their country's petroleum in 1938 and has since become the world's second-largest oil exporter. It has a state religion, so citizens must adhere to Islam

T.H. & Pam

and pledge loyalty to the king. Targets of discrimination include foreign civilians and Westerners affiliated with its oil-based economy. Because of the situation there, Tom unfortunately wasn't able to educate them like he wanted to.

Tom stayed active with teaching, politics, and GPA conventions. Sometimes his kids got to tag along to accompany him. These experiences helped him discern that he wanted to have a more active role in the industry. He would have to strike out on his own…again. All three of his sons plus all his former employees were still working for the previous company. He rented a corner of the MidFirst Bank building at 71st and Yale with consulting in mind.

BOLIVIA

Bolivia is a landlocked country with a varied terrain of mountains, desert, and rain forest. It is a sovereign state populated by multiple ethnicities and largely tribal. The country was importing gasoline, propane, and other hydrocarbon fuels to meet domestic demand. This required paying the market price, then subsidizing the cost to industrial and residential consumers. A processing plant would not only make Bolivia more self-sufficient, but would also allow for exports and create many jobs for locals.

Exporting tin had been their major source of income until the 1980s. The price of tin collapsed as aluminum became a less expensive alternative for making cans, pots, and pans. Suddenly, petroleum became Bolivia's primary moneymaker. It has the second-largest natural gas reserves discovered in South America. Out in the jungle, they needed a plant to produce propane. It would be going to a rural area where it was a high commodity, because that is what all the impoverished locals use for heating, cooking, fueling motors, generating electricity, and so forth.

The liquid that comes out of the ground is commonly called "raw" gasoline. It can be put through a reformer unit with a platinum catalyst under very high pressures and high temperatures. This transforms the raw fuel into a higher-octane gasoline that is used for cars. Propane is a by-product of this process. It can also be produced as a biofuel and is sold commercially in Europe.

This wasn't something Tom had done in the past. Routine gas plant business is referred to as "rope, soap, and dope," meaning hoisting materials, cleaning, and the grease that keeps gears running smoothly. He enlisted the help of his friend Larry Grimm, who had dealt more in the refinery business.

"We trust you to build this plant, Thomas. Can you do it?"

Never one to back down from a challenge, he answered, "You bet!" and got right to work on the design.

Susan (his daughter-in-law) was his first employee. She helped him get set up. Mike Pollard applied to be his Chief Financial Officer. "I can't afford you, Mike. It wouldn't be fair to you. I just have a few people helping out on this one project," Tom said, declining his application.

"I will work for you for nothing, Tom. Let's do this," Mike replied.

Tom called Matt. "I need your structural steel forte!" he said.

"I need a paycheck, and I'm working on things," Matt answered.

"Good, I'll see you in thirty minutes," Tom retorted. Matt fired up his Harley and headed over.

"When can you get here to manage this project, Glenn?" Tom asked.

"I'm subcontracted and am working on a project," Glenn answered.

"Good, finish it up, and I'll see you in two weeks," T.H. confirmed. "Neal, I need you over here for quality control," he continued.

Neal thought, "Why not, I'm in!" He had learned to stay out of the office and out of the way, preferring the shop and field for problem-solving. He was the liaison for the office.

Over the next few months, others joined Tom. He said, "Here's the deal. I'm going to form a company, and you guys can be part of it. We have a big project in Bolivia that I've been working on. I need all of your help." They were doing the work of a team triple their size. The new company opened a shop at the Port of Catoosa, after once again renting shop space from Big Jim for a while.

On location in Bolivia, Neal had to learn to say "alto" (meaning "stop") when he was being hoisted up out of the huge pressure vessels. There was a gate around the plant, and due to political unrest, the Americans weren't allowed outside of the jobsite. Protests erupted and reached a peak in 2003 with the "Gas War," centering on the country's vast natural gas reserves. The country had just recovered from similar protests regarding their water supply and tin mines.

Menu

LOUGH
eSKe
CASTLE

The Ladies and Gentlemen of Lough Eske Castle
Would like to welcome

The Russell Family

Carpaccio of Beetroot & Mandarin Orange
Gortnamona Goat's Cheese, Candied Walnut, Arugula, Basil Pesto

Donegal Smoked Haddock Galette
Yellow Bell Pepper, Aioli, Acorn Relish, Mesclun

Cauliflower Veloute
Madras Curry Crème Fraiche, Chives, Granny Smith Apple Brunoise

~ · ~

Pan-fried Cod
Crushed Roby Potato, Grilled Asparagus, White Wine Sauce

Lamb Shank
Mashed Potato, Root Vegetables

Traditional Turkey & Ham
Mash Potato, Roasted Vegetables & Cranberry Sauce

~ · ~

Homemade Apple Pie
Custard, Vanilla Bean Ice-cream

Passion Fruit Panna Cotta,
Sweet Lemon Sauce with Raspberries

Chocolate Sponge Mousse
Raspberry Jelly and Caramel Sauce

~ · ~

Freshly Brewed Tea or Coffee & Petit Fours

Betting on the Ferret Race in Scotland –
Tom, Neal, Glenn, Susan, Caitlyn.

In typical style, Tom and his employees were present for the start-up and to make sure the local plant operators were educated and going to be okay with their new plant.

Tom had to don a disguise to get out of the country. He put on a dirty shirt, a poncho, and a hat and made it onto a local workers' bus. His roommate couldn't contain his excitement that they had made it this far and was standing at the bus stop, waving good-bye, almost blowing his cover. Tom had to sit on the bus with his head down and not wave good-bye to his friends. When they passed villages, he could see they had used plywood from the jobsite to patch their homes. There were little stickers all over the village houses that said, *"Thomas Russell Company."* The company was not only providing them with valuable energy resources but also valuable housing resources! The checkpoints were tense but he had inherited the ability to keep his head down, focus on the job and not tout his identity.

In 2005 under Hormando Vaca Diez, President of the Senate of Bolivia, the Hydrocarbons Law was passed. The new law returned legal ownership of all hydrocarbons and natural resources like tin to the state (from it being privatized), with eighteen percent royalties and taxed at thirty-two percent. That meant the government had control of this valuable resource and revenue.

During the Bolivia job, Tom and the others remembered how much they enjoyed doing what they do and doing it with each other. Some other employees came aboard, and they started bidding on jobs and got some small ones. While Tom's competitors were trying to emulate Tom's earlier success at modular (skid-mounting) designs, he

Sophia and Pam hiking

was rolling full steam ahead. They built for Scissor Tail Energy and OKC, trying to reestablish connections, trust, and a niche above other processing plant manufacturers.

The doors didn't really begin to open until around 2005 and four significant plants later. Tom worked nonstop, and his co-workers followed suit. If there was ever any problem with a plant, Tom would say, "Get on a plane and go fix it, no matter if it's still under warranty or not." Tom didn't play invoice games, such as hanging on to people's cash to accrue more interest. People got paid on time. It was long hours and short deadlines. Profit from a plant was ten to fifteen percent, period!

A Country Girl Will Survive

Starting a business and getting it going is always risky. Again, times were tough needless to say. Tom's reputation was on the line. To have a support system was essential. Pam was the right woman for the job. Having been a single mom with a minor child still at home, she knew sacrificial love too well. Tom was "pounding the pavement" trying to get business and she had to hold down the fort at home.

It was not only their family, but many others were depending on them. They held people's trust and loyalty in the palms of their hands. Tom and Pam's faith was in their belief that they all stood under the protection of God's hand.

A customer in Mississippi was having some problems, so Tom went straight down to walk them through it. That night, Tom told Glenn to "set our alarm clock for 4:30 am."

"But our flight isn't until 9:00, and the plant is running," Glenn said.

"Our follow-up visit is before our flight home, son. That's what you do." He didn't hand out Band-Aids. He gave total attention to the person or task at hand.

As business picked up, he changed his company from using mostly subcontractors to having salaried employees and giving them ownership shares. In 2009, however, the pace slowed down, and the energy industry suffered another of its cyclical busts. In typical Tom style, he saw the positive potential of using downtime constructively to "retool." One of his retooling ideas was to have the son of an electrical engineer intern.

Mr. Joseph James, an electrical engineer, had started up over one hundred and thirty plants, and over one hundred of them were Tom's. Joe's expertise was developing the computer programs to control the plant operation. The program told pumps to start and valves to open or close. It also communicated when to measure the quantity and quality of the gas flowing through the plant.

Matt, Dave, Clint, and Tom golfing in Ireland.

Matt arranged for Mr. James's son, Joseph, Jr., who had disabilities, to intern two summers at the company. Mr. James credits that time and attention Matt showed his son as what "helped him transition to adult life and graduate from TU in mechanical engineering." Mr. James would eventually go on to start his own company, J.S. James Company.

Besides mentoring during the downturn, the company worked on making their standard modules even more adaptable, while other companies were laying off their people. Say a plant is producing 100 million cubic feet per day, but then you move it to another field that has twenty-percent richer gas. Tom realized there were common main components that might be slightly undersized or oversized if you moved them to a different location. What the company did was design plants of different sizes, which could be mixed and matched. Then the challenge wasn't "how big can we make it," it was "what truck is big enough for this to fit on?"

Compact, Underground Plant

A unique challenge came along at the airport in Denver, Colorado. They needed a deicer recycling plant and they needed it to be not only compact, but underground. So with a need requiring this kind of innovation, they called Thomas Russell Co.

So, when the airplane rolls onto a platform it is sprayed down with orange fluid, that is glycol. It chemically binds to the ice and melts it. All the liquid drains through the vents into Tom's regeneration plant.

There it heats up to a boil. Some steam evaporates into the air, the water and the glycol are separated and filtered. The glycol can then be regenerated and used again. After some time, the airport called and needed a new exchanger on it. "Go out and get them up and running again," Tom ordered.

* * *

"Think of a Mr. Potato Head toy. You can pull out and plug in pieces, change all the parts around, and they fit to create a different head that's doing the same thing," Neal explains in layman's terms. We are talking standardized, skid-mounted plants that can handle a range of gas analysis and provide the right products, as well as easily replace parts. This extended a plant's life by up to four times, giving all the other cats a run for their money. It met customer needs without reinventing the wheel. They could assure the customers that if they bought their plants, when gas flow went up, this plant could handle it. If you wanted to move it, this plant could handle it.

The Great Recession, beginning in 2008, caused the oil and gas industry to dry up for a whole year. Tom had to cut salaries, starting at the top. He cut his salary 40% and the other engineers' by 25%. "The oil and gas industry is cyclical. We will be back in business, so use this time wisely. Do your rainy-day projects, keep improving the designs, and stay busy," he assured the company. Having been through many ups and downs, he knew the right way was not to lay off and then have to rehire and retrain staff. Tom had raised his expectations by having stockholders. "As owners, it is up to us to sacrifice for the good of the company," he reiterated to them.

As soon as the oil and gas business picked up, they were in the position to get ahead of the competition. Tom also applied his innovation of standardized refrigeration plants to cryogenic plants (like putting Lego pieces together). An increased need for ethane arose. It is used to make plastics, antifreeze, detergents, food-ripening agents, and welding gas. If natural gas is cooled to −150°F, the ethane turns to liquid and seeps right out. Tom called on his ole friend J.L. Davis. "If I'm ever going to sell a cryo-plant, you are going to have to buy it from me," he said.

"I was just sitting here thinking, 'I sure do need a cryo-plant! Haha, whatever you are selling, Tom, I'll take one!" Jimmy answered.

Shale and Selling Slots

Things picked up by 2010, and then the market went crazy!
With such versatile and rugged designs, the company would
already be building plants in the shop before they were
even sold. The shale gas industry was highly invested now,
especially in West Virginia, Montana, and the Dakotas. Oil
prices went from $10 up to $50 a barrel! The U.S., Canada,
and China are the only producers of shale gas in commercial
quantities. Thanks to computers, geologists can now map
underground gas reserves much more accurately. They can
"see" natural gas trapped within the shale formations.

Shale rock has low matrix permeability, which means
you have to bust through it horizontally with water, sand,
and chemicals injected at a very high pressure to get
the product in commercial quantities (fracking). Some
analysts expect that shale gas will greatly expand the
worldwide energy supply by up to 46%. Since natural gas
burns much cleaner than coal, President Obama endorsed
development in 2012 to help reduce greenhouse emissions.

The company's innovative designs and the exploding
gas market went together like peas and carrots. Tom

hired Lamar Seale to manage sales. The Thomas Russell Company was booked out for two years. Everyone was working very long hours just to keep pace. It was a transition for the drafters to have to piece off their drawings when they were used to completing it before handing it over. Shop capacity expanded, and more engineers, drafters, and managers were hired. With up to sixty employees in the office, they occupied three floors. Quality plants were being delivered 27.5% faster than the competition.

Tower of Power

The company got a fractionator job from a customer they had been building plants for. It was almost above their capability but not their aspirations. "Can you do it?" the customer asked. "You bet!" Tom answered.

Most of the plant was built in the Catoosa shop. The tower was built in Houston, then put on barges to move it down the inner coastal channel and up the Mississippi River. The remaining six miles of dry land required a special heavy-duty trailer. The Tower weighed one million pounds! Standing it up was scary, but once in place, it was a beautiful sight…in the gas processing business.

Transporting The Tower

Installing The Tower

I just do the right thing and sometimes it pays off.

– Tom Russell

Chapter 10

LEGACY

TU Alumni Award 2013

"Blessed" is the answer Tom Russell gives to the question of "How would you describe your life?" From his modest beginnings in a large Irish-Catholic family to starting up not one but two incredibly successful businesses of his own, he credits all his good fortune to his strong faith, his supportive family, and his unyielding perseverance. Tom and Pam's endowments and scholarships offer others the same opportunities he has had to others. "I never envisioned myself reaching this status," he claims.

RETIREMENT

Fr. Webb and Tom

At the age of 81, after a decade of running his second company, Tom and the other shareholders decided to sell and retire in 2015. He became active in the Church again. He regularly attends Mass and religious observances at Christ the King Parish. He enjoys Father Elkin's (Pastor) and Father Webb's (Associate Pastor) homilies, then brunch with family. In 2017 he donated to CTK's centennial campaign, expanding faith enrichment rooms for the

Tom, Clint, Mandy and now Bishop Mueggenborg

Fr. Elkin

influx of young people and a growing community of over 1,400 families.

"What does Monsignor mean?" he once asked Father Mueggenborg (now Bishop of Seattle).

"It means it's time for us to go have a beer, Tom. It's just a title," he answered.

Tom is also a donor to Catholic Charities and Catholic Answers.

Tom and Pam enjoy traveling the world with friends and family; TU, OSU, and Dallas Cowboy football games; and spending time with grandkids. "Pam has been my best friend," Tom says, beaming. "She magically blended our families together with gatherings and trips.

She is the glue, and I love her for it." The last all-family vacation count was thirty-one people, eighteen of them grandchildren and two great-grandchildren.

Pam, your support and

Pam and her daughter Ashley

Tom and Pam enjoying family, authentic food, and each other.

special touch have reached many. Causes close to her heart are people on the North side, children, women in prison, and her faithful dogs, recently adopting a new puppy. She has a heart made of gold and reflects the love of Jesus everywhere she goes. Pam, we could not have done it without you. On behalf of your husband, your children and grandchildren, "the lifetime achievement" award goes to you!

The whole family in Ireland.

TU Russell School of Chemical Engineering, 2015

Tom and Pam have always believed in giving back and helping others along. They donated to renovate the expansion of classrooms at TU and improve laboratories for other students. Pam also previously contributed to TU's Department of Communicative Disorders, creating a vestibule in Stephenson Hall. Tom says he owes a lot of his success to TU because he received such a good education there. Also,

Tom being presented his plague from then TU president Dr. Gerard Clancy.

when he sold his company, he had five chemical engineers working for him that were TU graduates.

Tom recognized his professor A. Paul Buthod, who had such an impact on him, with an endowment chair as well as scholarships. The veteran's center in Calvin's name shows how Tom respects his mentors. When Tom received the honor of the Russell School of Chemical Engineering, he read thank-you notes from the podium that students had sent him about the doors that had been opened for them. As usual, he prefers to talk about other people's success.

GPA Lifetime Achievement Award, 2015

In San Antonio, the GPA honored "industry legend Tom Russell for Lifetime Achievement." They explained how he had dedicated fifty-five years to the industry, built

and sold two thriving companies, designed and built hundreds of plants, presented numerous papers, and served on the board of directors. He didn't just belong, he got involved. He improved society and the environment.

Tom and his supportive wife, Pam.

"His cryogenic processing units could handle a variety of natural gas volumes and richness levels. The standardization concept allowed customers to order plants not yet knowing where they were going or what their gas makeup would be," President and CEO Mark Sutton said during Tom's introduction.

Dad, you have a lot of friends and family who honor you with lifetime achievement for not only your professional accomplishments but also your personal character and the positive impact you have made on the world. The GPA announced that they considered themselves "lucky to be in his company," and so does anyone else who has ever had the pleasure of meeting you! We love you, and we know we can always come to you for mercy.

"Try not to be so unruly" Susan jokes. "You English have been oppressing us Irish for 800 years" Matt returns. With a laugh, off they go to explore!!!

Matt

Fly, boat, and bike around the world
Create things in your shop

Love, Dad

Jennifer helping
Audrey ride
her horse.

Alex & Glenn
serving community.

Glenn,

Fish and farm
Build an equestrian center

Love, Dad

Captain Russell

Fishing with friends and family.

Neal

Fish and fly planes
Work the land and preserve the creek

Love, Dad

Bryn,

Be the first Russell grandson
Entrepreneur Pelagos Custom
Appreciate outdoors like senior

Love, Papa & Pops

THE BRADLEY BUNCH

Bob was a combat fighter pilot during WWII and the
Korean War. He received the Distinguished Flying Cross
for his efforts in the Korean War. He was a V.P. of print
services at Pennwell and long-time member of Christ
the King Parish. He was the first inductee into the CTK
Hall of Fame! Bob and Mary were both inducted into the
Bishop Kelley Hall of Fame. The Bradley Charitable Trust
has helped many. Their son, Father Richard Bradley, was
ordained a priest in 1981 and is the pastor at St. Pius X.

THE McKEE MACHINE

Calvin retired as President of Warren Petroleum. The Republic of France knighted him for his service with

the U.S. 101st Airborne, which liberated France from the Nazis in WWII. His son Brian McKee co-owns Millennium, a missile defense company. One of their rockets is on display in the Smithsonian. Pat was very involved at the Church of the Madalene.

224

THE FUNKY MONKEYS

Bob Funk served in the South Pacific as a Navy Seabee in WWII. He endured the malaria he contracted there

for the rest of his life. He was a manager at Pennwell. He and Eileen were lifelong members of the Church of the Madalene. Bob was

involved with singing in the choir and the men's club. They were both involved in sports. When Bob wasn't enjoying writing poetry, he attended TU football games with Tom. Becky works for the Diocese.

Joe, Pat, Eileen, Pam & Tom, and Mary Ellen

Smoking Joe

Joe was a member of the priesthood from 1962–69 in
St. Louis. With the second Vatican Council, he decided to
change vocations and serve in other ways. He co-authored
a book in 1970 called *Wage Price Freeze*. It was regarding
President Nixon's ninety-day freeze on wages and prices to
counter inflation. Joe worked for FEMA disaster relief for
twenty-three years. He is an active member of Our Lady
Queen Catholic Parish and an avid reader.

Legacy Companies

Carlos M. Conerly (President of Natural Gas and Refining
Division at Linde) worked for Tom for over twenty years
as well as at APSI, Hanover, and Exterran. He remembers
most the advice that Tom gave him regarding customer
satisfaction. There was an incident with a glycol reboiler
in the shop that needed repair. When it was disassembled,
they discovered the tubes were corroded. The client had
failed to monitor the acidity of the glycol, and the plant
was no longer under warranty. Tom told him, "Fix it. Don't
argue fault or repair cost. Get them back online as soon as
possible." That same client later purchased many more gas
plants from Russell Company.

Carlos and Mark Helm recall when T.H. would
rush to the airport with a bid in hand to catch the next
plane out to meet with the customer in person. Often
the car would still be running! This often landed the job.
One year when business was dry for all, including the
field construction and shop employees, Tom went out to
the jobsite before Christmas and unexpectedly handed
out $100 bills to all his employees in the field. They

might not have had a project to work on, but he made sure they had Christmas.

Jaime Barraza (President of ISTI) asked Tom to send a letter of reference for him to build a cryogenic plant. Jaime needed the Energy Transfer customer to be confident in his ability to get the job done. Tom didn't write a letter. He said, "We're going to Texas." Tom took Jaime and some key members from his company to personally vouch for him. No further discussion was needed, and Jaime was awarded the job. They were treated to lunch, and a stream of people who had heard that Tom was in the building came by to meet him and shake his hand. It was Tom's plants that were performing so well for them. Mr. Barraza credits Tom's actions "above and beyond my wildest dreams, and he changed the course of my company forever that day."

Derrick Oneal (President of D.O. Company, LLC), fresh out of TU when he went to work for Tom, credits him with not only professional advice but also life lessons. "He encouraged me to always look for the positive." Mr. Oneal knew that he could approach Tom, but he also knew to have a solution (not just questions) ready and to

Grand opening of Gathering Place

be able to defend it. He and his wife graciously attended Tom's Russell School of Chemical Engineering naming.

GATHERING PLACE, 2018

On the east bank of the Arkansas River, George Kaiser has made it possible for Tulsa to have a world-class, public, hundred-acre park. When Tom and Pam got the call inviting them to be donors, they were thrilled with the concept of a unifying place for people to come together outdoors "in love and harmony." Tom had often taken his kids to the river for bicycling, roller-skating,

Grand Opening of Gathering Place

and walking. Tulsa hadn't seen anything like this since Orcutt Park in 1910.

The grand opening was such an enthusiastic occasion, with Tulsa's fortieth Mayor G.T. Bynum in attendance, speakers, music, mingling, and finding Tom and Pam's donation plaque on the wall. This historical event is the largest private gift to a public park in U.S. history! This park has been credited with being the #1 New Attraction in America, according to *USA Today*. Planned in 2020 is a Children's Museum with "critical thinking and creativity" activities.

More than thirty-nine Native American tribes inhabit Oklahoma. Gathering Place hosts the most comprehensive Native American festival powwow with music, dance, art, food, and ethnic dress. Tulsa and the tribes have long been proud of their native heritage. Each nation is able to present their story and speak about their cultural legacy. Visitors are able to purchase from the tribal vendors at the park as well as experience and share in their culture. It was important to Tom

Marquette students testing the park.

and Pam to be a part of something so unifying for the city. One can even play street hockey there!

Well, folks, Tom and Pam would love to stay and chat, but adventure awaits out there. The best part of this story is just beginning...

an irish blessing

May the road rise up to meet you.

May the wind be always at your back.

May the sun shine warm upon your face; the rains

fall soft upon your fields and until we meet again,

may God hold you in the palm of His hand.